THE SATIRIC VOICE

THE SATIRIC VOICE

ALBERT R. KITZHABER
General Editor

STODDARD MALARKEY
Literature Editor

BARBARA DRAKE

HOLT, RINEHART AND WINSTON, INC.
New York · Toronto · London · Sydney

ISBN: 0-03-010916-7

3456789 071 987654321

This text comprises the section "The Satiric Voice" from *Viewpoints in Literature*, copyright © 1974 by Holt, Rinehart and Winston, Inc.

Illustration credits appear in the back on page v.

ACKNOWLEDGMENTS

The authors and publisher have made every effort to trace the ownership of all selections found in this book and to make full acknowledgment for their use. Many of the selections are in the public domain.

Grateful acknowledgment is made to the following authors, publishers, agents, and individuals for their permission to reprint copyrighted material.

THE NEW YORK TIMES COMPANY, for "The Disposable Man" by Russell Baker. Copyright © 1965 by The New York Times Company. Reprinted by permission.

CHARLES SCRIBNER'S SONS, CHATTO AND WINDUS LTD., AND THE LITERARY ESTATE OF RING LARDNER, for "I Can't Breathe" from *Round Up* by Ring Lardner. Copyright 1926 by International Magazines Co., Inc., renewed copyright 1954 by Ellis A. Lardner. Reprinted by permission.

COWLES COMMUNICATIONS, INC., AND LEO ROSTEN, for "An Open Letter to the Mayor of New York" by Leo Rosten, from the February 12, 1963 issue of *Look Magazine.* Copyright © 1963 by Cowles Communications, Inc. Reprinted by permission.

REPRESENTATIVE ED FOREMAN for "Letter from a West Texas Constituent" by J. B. Lee (March 20, 1963). Reprinted by permission.

THE WORLD PUBLISHING COMPANY, for "The Vertical Negro Plan" from *Only in America* by Harry Golden. Copyright 1944, 1948, 1949, 1951, 1953, 1954, © 1955, 1956, 1957, 1958 by Harry Golden. Reprinted by permission.

LITTLE, BROWN AND COMPANY AND CURTIS BROWN LTD., for "Love Under the Republicans (or Democrats)" from *Verses from 1929 On* by Ogden Nash. Copyright 1930 by Ogden Nash. Originally appeared in *The New Yorker.* Reprinted by permission.

LITTLE, BROWN AND COMPANY, J. M. DENT & SONS LTD., AND CURTIS BROWN, LTD., for "A Bas Ben Adhem" from *Verses from 1929 On* by Ogden Nash. Copyright 1931 by Ogden Nash. Reprinted by permission.

ALFRED A. KNOPF, INC., AND ANDRE DEUTSCH LTD., for "The American Man—What of *Him?*" from *Assorted Prose* by John Updike. Copyright © 1956 by John Updike. Originally appeared in *The New Yorker.* Reprinted by permission.

INTRODUCTION

If imitation is the sincerest form of flattery, surely satire is the sharpest form of criticism. To criticize is merely to complain; to satirize is to hold up to public view, in a striking and clever way, some of the failings and follies of man.

The basic element of satire is wit; the satirist pokes fun at people, at events, at attitudes, often in the hope of bringing about a change.

In this book, you will read a number of satiric pieces. All of them should amuse you; perhaps some of them will inspire you to take a closer look at yourself and the world around you.

CONTENTS

Contents

Le Charivari: M. Babinet Prévenu par Sa Portière de la Visite de la Comète, By Honoré Daumier, 1858.

The Satiric Voice

Mixing humor with criticism may seem a little like trying to mix oil with water. Yet this is the kind of mixture that the satirist achieves. At the same time he is making us smile or laugh, he is telling us that something is wrong. He may even be pointing an accusing finger at *you*.

To understand how humor and criticism can be combined, consider your own experience. Have you even been in an argument that suddenly disintegrated into laughter? If so, it probably happened because you and your opponent suddenly saw yourselves in a satirical light—you saw the ridiculousness of what you were arguing about, or you realized the absurdity of the argument itself and the way you were behaving. Or, when

1

you have done something embarrassing and are busy criticizing yourself, has someone else ever pointed out the humor in what you have done? If so, that person has helped you to see yourself as a satirist might see you. Recognizing the humor, the incongruity, or the absurdity in an action which also deserves criticism is the essence of the satiric view. The satirist, master of this blend of criticism and humor, suggests reform, but he usually evokes a chuckle as well.

The word "satire" evolved from the Latin word *satura*, meaning "full" and also referring to a bowl of mixed fruits or a salad. As you read these selections, you may well picture the writers as salad-makers, adding a pinch of this, some bits of that, and stirring the whole mixture into a highly seasoned delicacy.

Traditionally, satire was classified according to two basic types, named after the Roman satirists Horace and Juvenal. "Horatian" satire is light and amusing, whereas "Juvenalian" satire is bitter and shocking. But between these two extremes lies a vast range of attitudes; amusement and contempt may be blended in varying proportions. You might imagine these two qualities as the oil and the vinegar in a salad dressing, differing in proportion according to the chef's taste.

We use the term "satire" to designate a distinct type of literature. However, unlike poems and short stories, which are called poems or stories according to the way they are put together, satires are so named because of the way the author treats his subject. Poems, stories, essays, novels, and plays may be satires, but they are still poems, stories, essays, novels, and plays. In other words, satire is a matter of *point of view*, rather than form.

Like any other writer, the satirist has an infinite number of subjects at his disposal. As you read, you will see how the satirist's tone will vary according to the seriousness of his subject. For instance, a young girl's romantic silliness is suitable for treatment in the Horatian manner, whereas a social condition which permits people to suffer in abject poverty is appropriate for treatment in the Juvenalian manner. Politics and politicians are natural objects of both kinds of satire.

Jonathan Swift, the well-known satirist who wrote *Gulliver's Travels*, put some of his thoughts on satire into verse:

> Perhaps I may allow, the Dean
> Had too much Satyr in his Vein;
> And seemed determined not to starve it,
> Because no Age could more deserve it.

Yet, Malice never was his Aim;
He lash'd the Vice but spar'd the Name.
No Individual could resent,
Where thousands equally were meant.
His Satyr points at no Defect,
But what all Mortals may correct.

Swift says that the satirist should aim his satire where it will do the most good — at responsible parties and correctable faults. He demands, too, that satire not descend into petty backbiting or mudslinging.

If a satire is well done, if it really comes close to the truth about human beings and social systems, we can usually appreciate its meaning long after the specific person or group who inspired the satire is forgotten. Consider as an illustration the following statement by lawyer and author Clarence Darrow: "When I was a boy I was told that anyone could become President; I'm beginning to believe it." Darrow had a specific president in mind, but anyone familiar with the log-cabin tradition of democratic government who has seen someone other than his own favorite candidate elected can appreciate the ironic intent of Darrow's remark without knowing exactly whom Darrow had in mind.

On the other hand, it is also true that the person who knows exactly what or whom the satirist has in mind is likely to enjoy and appreciate the satire more. This is particularly true of *caricatures,* in which the satirist focuses upon specific persons, exaggerating and distorting their features and characteristics. The newspapers are full of caricatures in the form of political cartoons. But unless one knows something about the object of the caricature, the humor is usually lost on him. For that reason, most of the satires included in this section are not caricatures of specific individuals but ironic commentaries on social trends and events which should not be difficult for you to understand.

The following selections are arranged according to the way in which the satirist presents his material. In the first group are *satiric monologues,* in which you will "hear" the author speaking, usually with an ironic tone, in a voice which is more or less his own. In the second group you will read *parodies,* satiric imitations of other well-known pieces of writing. The last group contains *satiric narratives.* In each group, you will find that some of the satires are more direct in their criticism than others. As you read, consider the advantage of *indirection* in this kind of writing.

SATIRIC MONOLOGUES

The term *monologue* applies to any speech or piece of writing in which just one speaker delivers all of the material. According to this definition, many short stories, poems, and novels are monologues, and essays are almost always monologues. In a monologue, the question of technical point of view is easily settled—there is just one speaker, he speaks in the first person, and he is easy to identify. However, when a monologue is also a *satire*, the point of view becomes a little more complicated. Satirists seldom say exactly what they mean; they exaggerate, they use irony, they are sarcastic, often saying just the opposite of what they mean.

Depending upon how the satirist chooses to handle his speaker, the satiric voice may come through in a variety of ways. For instance, one satirist may speak in his own voice. He may exaggerate, he may use irony, but because he makes his attitude quite clear, there is little question about the object of his satire. Another satirist, choosing to be less direct, may assume a false identity. By pretending to be someone else, usually a person quite different from himself, he can achieve certain effects that he could not achieve otherwise. A third satirist may don an *ironic* mask. In order to shock his audience into sympathy with his real attitudes, he may state —as absolute truth—views which are the exact opposite of what he really believes. Here we find *indirection* at its best.

In the following pages you will find examples of each of these three approaches. As you read, consider how the voice of the speaker is particularly appropriate to the satirist's purposes.

Never before has the world seen such a complicated array of products manufactured for the sole purpose of making life simpler. Most of us think of material progress as a good thing. But perhaps man needs to struggle a little in order to lead a meaningful life. Baker's opening reference to the "stingless bee" is particularly appropriate. What happens to life when the "sting" is removed?

The Disposable Man

Russell Baker

How far is American know-how from producing a disposable man?

Closer perhaps than it seems. Sears, Roebuck and Company is already marketing a stingless bee, for people who want to keep bees without really being bothered. The stingless bee, of course, was inevitable, just as the disposable man is. It is merely the latest in a long line of technological breakthroughs that have brought us into the Nothing Generation or, as social psychologists might call it, the Non Age.

The Less Life

The purpose of the Non Age is to make it possible for the Nothing Generation to get through a complete non-life without any of the untidy bothers of living, like bee stings. Hence, the non-bee.

Other adjuncts of the good non-life include the fuzzless peach, the seedless grape, and odorless booze (vodka). All serve the same basic function as the stingless bee. They relieve man of the need to come to grips with nature by devising schemes to keep peach fuzz off his chin, seeds out of his appendix and neighbors from knowing that he is snockered.

The child of the Nothing Generation is naturally swaddled in a disposable diaper. As he grows he goes to the painless dentist. His father lives in a no-down-payment house and wears a wrinkle-free, drip-dry wardrobe. On formal occasions, he wears a clip-on tie.

The essence of non-life is non-involvement, more positively known as playing it safe. And so literature has created the anti-hero for the anti-theater and the anti-novel. The anti-hero sits around in garbage cans doing nothing for hours, except saying "no" to life and waiting to be disposed of.

He is a great favorite of the Nothing Generation, which can listen to him for hours, even on caffeine-free coffee.

Parenthood Without Pain

When the anti-hero wants to carbonate his stomach he takes a non-caloric soft drink. It comes in a disposable, no-deposit no-return bottle, or a throwaway can. For amusement he sits in dehumidified air watching non-actors perform non-dramas about non-people and absorbing advertisements that tell how to take the misery out of washday, the odors out of living and the challenge out of opening a milk can.

The beauty of the Non Age is that it makes non-life so easy, and creates so much leisure time to enjoy non-living. The throwaway bottle saves parents from the unpleasantness of seeing junior sulk when ordered to take the bottles back to the store. It also gives them a chance to worry each other about why junior has nothing to do with his time but wolf fuzzless peaches and seedless grapes.

The Non Age, fortunately, provides for junior, should the non-life hang heavily on his hands and make him edgy. The doctor will prescribe some tranquilizers to keep him in a non-emotional state. The prescription will be written with a throwaway pen.

In this state junior may be induced to turn down the anti-music on the phonograph and turn his hand to something perfectly unchallenging, like keeping stingless bees.

What next in the march toward a better non-life for all Americans? The workless job is already well developed. The disposable conscience is old hat. There is room perhaps, as recent events in St. Augustine and Mississippi suggest, for the painless truncheon, though a case can be made that when safe, uninvolved non-living becomes absolute, everything will be painless.

No. What the Nothing Generation needs for self-completion is the disposable man. He will be able to pass from disposable diaper to the trash can, leaving no trace but an estate for his disposable children.

It will not take you long to discover that the speaker of the following monologue is not the author, nor would anyone imagine that the speaker is at all like him. As you read the diary of this passionate girl, you will realize that the author is not nearly so enamored of her as her many suitors are. Consider whether Lardner is attacking "the vice" or a particular individual. Does he consider the girl malicious, or simply silly? In spite of the fact that certain references place her in a different time than ours, you may find that she seems familiar.

I Can't Breathe

Ring Lardner

July 12

I am staying here at the Inn for two weeks with my Uncle Nat and Aunt Jule and I think I will keep a kind of diary while I am here to help pass the time and so I can have a record of things that happen though goodness knows there isn't lightly to anything happen, that is anything exciting with Uncle Nat and Aunt Jule making the plans as they are both at least 35 years old and maybe older.

Dad and mother are abroad to be gone a month and me coming here is supposed to be a recompence for them not taking me with them. A fine recompence to be left with old people that come to a place like this to rest. Still it would be a heavenly place under different conditions, for instance if Walter were here, too. It would be heavenly if he were here, the very thought of it makes my heart stop.

I can't stand it. I won't think about it.

This is our first separation since we have been engaged, nearly 17 days. It will be 17 days tomorrow. And the hotel orchestra at dinner this evening played that old thing "Oh how I miss you tonight" and it seemed as if they must be playing it for my benefit though of course the person in that song is talking about how they miss their mother though of course I miss mother too, but a person gets used to missing their mother and it isn't like Walter or the person you are engaged to.

But there won't be any more separations much longer, we are going to be married in December even if mother does laugh when I talk to her about it because she says I am crazy to even think of getting married at 18.

She got married herself when she was 18, but of course that was "different," she wasn't crazy like I am, she knew whom she was marrying. As if Walter were a policeman or a foreigner or something. And she says she was only engaged once while I have been engaged at least five times a year since I was 14, of course it really isn't as bad as that and I have really only been really what I call engaged six times altogether, but is getting engaged my fault when they keep insisting and hammering at you and if you didn't say yes they would never go home.

But it is different with Walter. I honestly believe if he had not asked me I would have asked him. Of course I wouldn't have, but I would have died. And this is the first time I have ever been engaged to be really married. The other times when they talked about when we should get married I just laughed at them, but I hadn't been engaged to Walter ten minutes when he brought up the subject of marriage and I didn't laugh. I wouldn't be engaged to him unless it was to be married. I couldn't stand it.

Anyway mother may as well get used to the idea because it is "No Foolin'" this time and we have got our plans all made and I am going to be married at home and go out to California and Hollywood on our honeymoon. December, five months away. I can't stand it. I can't wait.

There were a couple of awfully nice looking boys sitting together alone in the dining-room tonight. One of them wasn't so much, but the other was cute. And he——

There's the dance orchestra playing "Always," what they played at the Biltmore the day I met Walter. "Not for just an hour not for just a day." I can't live. I can't breathe.

July 13

This has been a much more exciting day than I expected under the circumstances. In the first place I got two long night letters, one from Walter and one from Gordon Flint. I don't see how Walter ever had the nerve to send his, there was everything in it and it must have been horribly embarrassing for him while the telegraph operator was reading it over and counting the words to say nothing of embarrassing the operator.

But the one from Gordon was a kind of a shock. He just got back from a trip around the world, left last December to go on it and got back yesterday and called up our house and Helga gave him my address, and his telegram, well it was nearly as bad as Walter's. The trouble is that Gordon and I were engaged when he went away, or at least he thought so and he wrote to me right along all the time he was away and sent cables and things and for a while I answered his letters, but then I lost track of his itinery and couldn't write to him any more and when I got really engaged to Walter I couldn't let Gordon know because I had no idea where he was besides not wanting to spoil his trip.

And now he still thinks we are engaged and he is going to call me up tomorrow from Chicago and how in the world can I explain things and get him to understand because he is really serious and I like him ever and ever so much and in lots of ways he is nicer than Walter, not really nicer but better looking and there is no comparison between their dancing. Walter simply can't learn to dance, that is really dance. He says it is because he is flat footed, he says that as a joke, but it is true and I wish to heavens it wasn't.

All forenoon I thought and thought and thought about what to say to Gordon when he calls up and finally I couldn't stand thinking about it any more and just made up my mind I wouldn't think about it any more. But I will tell the truth though it will kill me to hurt him.

I went down to lunch with Uncle Nat and Aunt Jule and they were going out to play golf this afternoon and were insisting that I go with them, but I told them I had a headache and then I had a terrible time getting them to go without me. I didn't have a headache at all and just wanted to be alone to think about Walter and besides when you play with Uncle Nat he is always correcting your stance or your swing or something and always puts his hands on my arms or shoulders to show me the right way and I can't stand it to have old men touch me, even if they are your uncle.

I finally got rid of them and I was sitting watching the tennis when that boy that I saw last night, the cute one, came and sat right next to me and of course I didn't look at him and I was going to smoke a cigarette and found I had left my lighter upstairs and I started to get up and go after it when all of a sudden he was offering me his lighter and I couldn't very well refuse it without being rude. So we got to talking and he is even cuter than he looks, the most original and wittiest person I believe I ever met and I haven't laughed so much in I don't know how long.

For one thing he asked me if I had heard Rockefeller's song and I said no and he began singing "Oil alone." Then he asked me if I knew the orange juice song and I told him no again and he said it was "Orange juice sorry you made me cry." I was in hysterics before we had been together ten minutes.

His name is Frank Caswell and he has been out of Dartmouth a year and is 24 years old. That isn't so terribly old, only two years older than Walter and three years older than Gordon. I hate the name Frank, but Caswell is all right and he is so cute.

He was out in California last winter and visited Hollywood and met everybody in the world and it is fascinating to listen to him. He met Norma Shearer and he said he thought she was the prettiest thing he had ever seen. What he said was "I did think she was the prettiest girl in the world, till today." I was going to pretend I didn't get it, but I finally told him to be sensible or I would never be able to believe anything he said.

Well, he wanted me to dance with him tonight after dinner and the next question was how to explain how we had met each other to Uncle Nat and Aunt Jule. Frank said he would fix that all right and sure enough he got himself introduced to Uncle Nat when Uncle Nat came in from golf and after dinner Uncle Nat introduced him to me and Aunt Jule too and we danced together all evening, that is not Aunt Jule. They went to bed, thank heavens.

He is a heavenly dancer, as good as Gordon. One dance we were dancing and for one of the encores the orchestra played "In a cottage small by a waterfall" and I simply couldn't dance to it. I just stopped still and said "Listen, I can't bear it, I can't breathe" and poor Frank thought I was sick or something and I had to explain that that was the tune the orchestra played the night I sat at the next table to Jack Barrymore at Barney Gallant's.

I made him sit out that encore and wouldn't let him talk till they got through playing it. Then they played something else and I was all right again and Frank told me about meeting Jack Barrymore. Imagine meeting him. I couldn't live.

I promised Aunt Jule I would go to bed at eleven and it is way past that now, but I am all ready for bed and have just been writing this. Tomorrow Gordon is going to call up and what will I say to him? I just won't think about it.

July 14

Gordon called up this morning from Chicago and it was wonderful to hear his voice again though the connection was terrible. He asked me if I still loved him and I tried to tell him no, but I knew that would mean an explanation and the connection was so bad that I never could make him understand so I said yes, but I almost whispered it purposely, thinking he wouldn't hear me, but he heard me all right and he said that made everything all right with the world. He said he thought I had stopped loving him because I had stopped writing.

I wish the connection had been decent and I could have told him how things were, but now it is terrible because he is planning to get to New York the day I get there and heaven knows what I will do because Walter will be there, too. I just won't think about it.

Aunt Jule came in my room just after I was through talking to Gordon, thank heavens. The room was full of flowers. Walter had sent me some and so had Frank. I got another long night letter from Walter, just as silly as the first one. I wish he would say those things in letters instead of night letters so everybody in the world wouldn't see them. Aunt Jule wanted me to read it aloud to her. I would have died.

While she was still in the room, Frank called up and asked me to play golf with him and I said all right and Aunt Jule said she was glad my headache was gone. She was trying to be funny.

I played golf with Frank this afternoon. He is a beautiful golfer and it is thrilling to watch him drive, his swing is so much more graceful than Walter's. I asked him to watch me swing and tell me what was the matter with me, but he said he couldn't look at anything but my face and there wasn't anything the matter with that.

He told me the boy who was here with him had been called home and he was glad of it because I might have liked him, the other boy, better than himself. I told him that couldn't be possible and he asked me if I really meant that and I said of course, but I smiled when I said it so he wouldn't take it too seriously.

We danced again tonight and Uncle Nat and Aunt Jule sat with us a while and danced a couple of dances themselves, but they were really there to get better acquainted with Frank and see if he was all right for me to be with. I know they certainly couldn't have enjoyed their own dancing, no old people really can enjoy it because they can't really *do* anything.

They were favorably impressed with Frank I think, at least Aunt Jule didn't say I must be in bed at eleven, but just not to stay up too late. I guess it is a big surprise to a girl's parents and aunts and uncles to find out that the boys you go around with are all right, they always seem to think that if I seem to like somebody and the person pays a little attention to me, why he must be a convict or a policeman or a drunkard or something queer.

Frank had some more songs for me tonight. He asked me if I knew the asthma song and I said I didn't and he said "Oh, you must know that. It goes yes, sir, asthma baby." Then he told me about the underwear song, "I underwear my baby is tonight." He keeps you in hysterics and yet he has his serious side, in fact he was awfully serious when he said good night to me and his eyes simply shown. I wish Walter were more like him in some ways, but I mustn't think about that.

July 15

I simply can't live and I know I'll never sleep tonight. I am in a terrible predicament or rather I won't know whether I really am or not till tomorrow and that is what makes it so terrible.

After we had danced two or three dances, Frank asked me to go for a ride with him and we went for a ride in his car and he had had some cocktails and during the ride he had some drinks out of a flask and finally he told me he loved me and I said not to be silly, but he said he was perfectly serious and he certainly acted that way. He asked me if I loved anybody else and I said yes and he asked if I didn't love him more than anybody else and I said yes, but only because I thought he had probably had too much to drink and wouldn't remember it anyway and the best thing to do was humor him under the circumstances.

Then all of a sudden he asked me when I could marry him and I said, just as a joke, that I couldn't possibly marry him before December. He said that was a long time to wait, but I was certainly worth waiting for and he said a lot of other things and maybe I humored him a little too much, but that is just the trouble, I don't know.

I was absolutely sure he was tight and would forget the whole thing, but that was early in the evening, and when we said good night he was a whole lot more sober than he had been and now I am not sure how it stands. If he doesn't remember anything about it, of course I am all right. But if he does remember and if he took me seriously, I will simply have to tell him about Walter and maybe about Gordon, too, And it isn't going to be easy. The suspense is what is maddening and I know I'll never live through this night.

July 16

I can't stand it, I can't breathe, life is impossible. Frank remembered everything about last night and firmly believes we are engaged and going to be married in December. His people live in New York and he says he is going back when I do and have them meet me.

Of course it can't go on and tomorrow I will tell him about Walter or Gordon or both of them. I know it is going to hurt him terribly, perhaps spoil his life and I would give anything in the world not to have had it happen. I hate so to hurt him because he is so nice besides being so cute and attractive.

He sent me the loveliest flowers this morning and called up at ten and wanted to know how soon he could see me and I hope the girl wasn't listening in because the things he said were, well, like Walter's night letters.

And that is another terrible thing, today I didn't get a night letter from Walter, but there was a regular letter instead and I carried it around in my purse all this afternoon and evening and never remembered to read it till ten minutes ago when I came up in the room. Walter is worried because I have only sent him two telegrams and written him one letter since I have been here, he would be a lot more worried if he knew what has happened now, though of course it can't make any difference because he is the one I am really engaged to be married to and the one I told mother I was going to marry in December and I wouldn't dare tell her it was somebody else.

I met Frank for lunch and we went for a ride this afternoon and he was so much in love and so lovely to me that I simply did not have the heart to tell him the truth, I am surely going to tell him tomorrow and telling him today would have just meant one more day of unhappiness for both of us.

He said his people had plenty of money and his father had offered to take him into partnership and he might accept, but he thinks his true vocation is journalism with a view to eventually writing novels and if I was willing to undergo a few hardships just at first we would probably both be happier later on if he was doing something he really liked. I didn't know what to say, but finally I said I wanted him to suit himself and money wasn't everything.

He asked me where I would like to go on my honeymoon and I suppose I ought to have told him my honeymoon was all planned, that I was going to California, with Walter, but all I said was that I had always wanted to go to California and he was enthusiastic and said that is where we would surely go and he would take me to Hollywood and introduce me to all those wonderful people he met there last winter. It nearly takes my breath away to think of it, going there with someone who really knows people and has the entrée.

We danced again tonight, just two or three dances, and then went out and sat in the tennis-court, but I came upstairs early because Aunt Jule had acted kind of funny at dinner. And I wanted to be alone, too, and think, but the more I think the worse it gets.

Sometimes I wish I were dead, maybe that is the only solution and it would be best for everyone concerned. I *will* die if things keep on the way they have been. But of course tomorrow it will be all over, with Frank I mean, for I must tell him the truth no matter how much it hurts us both. Though I don't care how much it hurts me. The thought of hurting him is what is driving me mad. I can't bear it.

July 18

I have skipped a day. I was busy every minute of yesterday and so exhausted when I came upstairs that I was tempted to fall into bed with all my clothes on. First Gordon called me up from Chicago to remind me that he would be in New York the day I got there and that when he comes he wants me all to himself all the time and we can make plans for our wedding. The connection was bad again and I just couldn't explain to him about Walter.

I had an engagement with Frank for lunch and just as we were going in another long distance call came, from Walter this time. He wanted to know why I haven't written more letters and sent him more telegrams and asked me if I still loved him and of course I told him yes because I really do. Then he asked if I had met any men here and I told him I had met one, a friend of Uncle Nat's. After all it was Uncle Nat who introduced me to Frank. He reminded me that he would be in New York on the 25th which is the day I expect to get home, and said he would have theater tickets for that night and we would go somewhere afterwards and dance.

Frank insisted on knowing who had kept me talking so long and I told him it was a boy I had known a long while, a very dear friend of mine and a friend of my family's. Frank was jealous and kept asking questions till I thought I would go mad. He was so serious and kind of cross and gruff that I gave up the plan of telling him the truth till some time when he is in better spirits.

I played golf with Frank in the afternoon and we took a ride last night and I wanted to get in early because I had promised both Walter and Gordon that I would write them long letters, but Frank wouldn't bring me back to the Inn till I had named a definite date in December. I finally told him the 10th and he said all right if I was sure that wasn't a Sunday. I said I would have to look it up but as a matter of fact I know the 10th falls on a Friday because the date Walter and I have agreed on for our wedding is Saturday the 11th.

Today has just been the same thing over again, two more night letters, a long distance call from Chicago, golf and a ride with Frank, and the room full of flowers. But tomorrow I am going to tell Frank and I am going to write Gordon a long letter and tell him, too, because this simply can't go on any longer. I can't breathe. I can't live.

July 21

I wrote to Gordon yesterday, but I didn't say anything about Walter because I don't think it is a thing a person ought to do by letter. I can tell him when he gets to New York and then I will be sure that he doesn't take it too hard and I can promise him that I will be friends with him always and make him promise not to do anything silly, while if I told it to him in a letter there is no telling what he would do, there all alone.

And I haven't told Frank because he hasn't been feeling well, he is terribly sunburned and it hurts him terribly so he can hardly play golf or dance, and I want him to be feeling his best when I do tell him, but whether he is all right or not I simply must tell him tomorrow because he is actually planning to leave here on the same train with us Saturday night and I can't let him do that.

Life is so hopeless and it could be so wonderful. For instance how heavenly it would be if I could marry Frank first and stay married to him five years and he would be the one who would take me to Hollywood and maybe we could go on parties with Norman Kerry and Jack Barrymore and Buster Collier and Marion Davies and Lois Moran.

And at the end of five years Frank could go into journalism and write novels and I would only be 23 and I could marry Gordon and he would be ready for another trip around the world and he could show me things better than someone who had never seen them before.

Gordon and I would separate at the end of five years and I would be 28 and I know of lots of women that never even got married the first time till they were 28 though I don't suppose that was their fault, but I would marry Walter then, for after all he is the one I really love and want to spend most of my life with and I wouldn't care whether he could dance or not when I was that old. Before long we would be as old as Uncle Nat and Aunt Jule and I certainly wouldn't want to dance at their age when all you can do is just hobble around the floor. But Walter is so wonderful as a companion and we would enjoy the same things and be pals and maybe we would begin to have children.

But that is all impossible though it wouldn't be if older people just had sense and would look at things the right way.

It is only half past ten, the earliest I have gone to bed in weeks, but I am worn out and Frank went to bed early so he could put cold cream on his sunburn.

Listen, diary, the orchestra is playing "Limehouse Blues." The first tune I danced to with Merle Oliver, two years ago. I can't stand it. And how funny that they should play that old tune tonight of all nights, when I have been thinking of Merle off and on all day and I hadn't thought of him before in weeks and weeks. I wonder where he is, I wonder if it is just an accident or if it means I am going to see him again. I simply mustn't think about it or I'll die.

July 22

I knew it wasn't an accident. I knew it must mean something, and it did.

Merle is coming here today, here to this Inn, and just to see me. And there can only be one reason. And only one answer. I knew that when I heard his voice calling from Boston. How could I ever had thought I loved anyone else? How could he ever have thought I meant it when I told him I was engaged to George Morse?

A whole year and he still cares and I still care. That shows we were always intended for each other and for no one else. I won't make *him* wait till December. I doubt if we even wait till dad and mother get home. And as for a honeymoon I will go with him to Long Beach or the Bronx Zoo, wherever he wants to take me.

After all this is the best way out of it, the only way. I won't have to say anything to Frank, he will guess when he sees me with Merle. And when I get home Sunday and Walter and Gordon call me up, I will invite them both to dinner and Merle can tell them himself, with two of them there it will only hurt each one half as much as if they were alone.

The train is due at 2:40, almost three hours from now. I can't wait. And what if it should be late? I can't stand it.

QUESTIONS FOR DISCUSSION

1. Why has Lardner written this satire in the form of a diary? What other form might he have used to create a similar effect?
2. How has Lardner made this seem like a real diary? What do the language, spelling, and organization suggest about the personality of the "writer"? Do the observations and sentiments expressed in the diary seem consistent with her character?
3. Extravagant exaggeration or overstatement is called *hyperbole*. The girl's frequent statement, "I can't breathe," is an example. Point to other examples in the diary. Why has the author used hyperbole in this satire?
4. What does the "writer" reveal about herself through the following items in her diary?
   a) She recognizes two kinds of engagement—one to be married, the other just to be engaged.
   b) She considers her aunt and uncle, at thirty-five, "maybe older," to be ancient and incapable of enjoying themselves at frivolous pastimes like dancing.
   c) She places great importance on "signs" and "omens" like the particular songs played by the orchestra.
   d) She would like to be married to each of her boyfriends at different times.
   e) She is afraid she is going to spoil Frank's whole life by not marrying him.

I Can't Breathe

5. Which of Frank's characteristics first attract her? What does this reveal about her?
6. To "rationalize" is to invent reasonable and satisfying explanations for our behavior when we do not want to admit our real reasons for what we do. Does this girl rationalize? Find specific examples.
7. Do you think the writer found a good solution to her problem at the end of her diary? How do you expect things to work out for her?
8. Why is the subject of "I Can't Breathe" particularly suitable for a monologue in which the satirist's victim reveals her *own* character? Is this particular girl the only object of Lardner's satire?

Although many New Yorkers love their city, New Yorkers as a whole are famous for their complaints. The following letter, which was *not* sent to the mayor, first appeared in Leo Rosten's column in *Look* magazine. The writer of the letter is a fictitious character, "J. R. Jukes." As you read, consider how the use of Jukes as the speaker helps Rosten achieve his purpose. What *is* his purpose?

An Open Letter to the Mayor of New York

Leo Rosten

1963

Dear Mr. Mayor:

There's a fellow I want to report—so's you can arrest him or deport him or what. He's a real troublemaker who goes around saying awful things about you. I think he's a Communist, or even a Republican.

Last night, whilst shooting the breeze, How do you like living in little old NY? he asks.

I like NY fine, I said.

He looks at me like I'm some kind of Astronut. I mean NY the capital of Noise, Dirt, Muggings and Holes in every street, he says. (Right there I should of realize this guy is carrying around some grudge to grind.)

How long, he asks, does it take you to commute to and fro your place of work?

I do not commute, I say, as I work only 30 blocks from here, in the Umpire State Bilding, which takes me 45 minutes to 1 hour.

If that ain't commuting I'd like to know what is, he says. How do you like our Mayor?

OK, I said. His heart's in the right place.

If his heart wasn't in the right place it couldn't pump enough blood to his head to keep him awake, he said, which there's no proof he is.

Ha, ha, ha, I argued.

Want a bargain in a gasmask? he said.

What do I want a gasmask for? I ask.

So's you can survive from the fumes, he says. Don't you know the pop. of NY is *being gassed to death* from the xhaust pipes of Trucks, Buses and Cars?

An Open Letter
to the Mayor
of New York

19

I told him I didn't notice, as I am from the soft-coal belt of Pa. —and back home people are kind of proud of the fact that we have the lowest oxygen rate in the entire USA.

O my, he groned. Do you realize that even air conditioners only last 4—5 years in NY, on account of the gas and acid fumes eat away the metal parts?

Well, I'm not an air conditioner, I said.

I hate to think what they will find when they open up *your* lungs, he said, assuming there are any lungs left to describe. Why can't the Mayor make every Truck, Bus and Car clean its filters and fix its carboretors?

You can't see your own xhaust fumes if you are driving, I said, as you drive in front whereas the xhaust pipes are in *back*.

That is why I am organizing a Committee, he said, so when a citizen sees a Bus, Truck or Car trying to kill people by poisoning the air, he slaps 1 of these stickers on the vehicle. (He shows me a sticker and you know what it says? So help me, Mayor, it says—

STOP POISONING YOUR FELLOW AMERICANS!
Your xhaust is black filth!
You are choking our lungs!
You are shriveling our leafs!

That won't do no good, I said. They will just scrape them stickers off.

In that case, we go into action! (Now he wips out a long Rubber Hose.) You attach 1 end to the xhaust pipe and stick the other end in the window, right next to the Driver's puss. If he loves fumes, let him breathe them!

What if the window ain't open? I said.

Brake it, he said simply.

I said, Braking car windows is a crime.

He said, Poisoning 8,000,000 NYorkers is a worse crime. Why, I went up to Conn. last week to visit a refugee from NY, and the fresh air there made me so sick they had to blow carbon monoxy in my face to revive me.

By now he looks ready to split a gut, so I decide to quiet him up. Why don't you write all these beefs, I ask, to Mayor Wagner in person?

He laughed so hard you could scramble eggs on his stomack. Write the *Mayor?* he strangles. I have already wrote that Boy Scout a dozen letters, and I get back a dozen replies from some stoodge, saying the Mayor has turned my complaints over to "the proper dept." Well, they are so proper they don't even answer — because we ain't been formally introduced. What do you do with your Old Rubbers?

I give them to the Salvation Army, I said.

What? he cries. You are suppose to take them to one of the bildings where they burn old rubber and hot-water bags in the incinerators. Why, old rubber is one of our finest products for making Smog and Smoke. I can see you are low in civic spirit, he says. I bet you ain't even been in Central Park resently.

Why should I go Central Park? I said.

So's you can be mugged like everyone else, he said, and push up our crime statistiks.

You don't have to go in Central Park to get mugged, I said. We have had 2 muggings, 3 break-ins and a stabbing right on this block.

That shows what a great Mayor we have, he said.

Ain't there even 1 good thing you can say about him? I challendged.

He closed his both eyes and took so long thinking I wondered is he coming down with the African Sleeping Sickness, which strikes without warning. Finally he said, I admit Wagner is doing more than any man alive to solve the Number 1 Problem of the World today — Do you know what the Number 1 Problem is?

Overweight, I said.

He groned. Try again.

Cavities, I said.

Lay down and rest, he says, you sure need it. The Number 1 Problem of the World is — OVERPOPULATION. And no one is doing more to reduce it than Bewildered Bob. As for NY, it's a race between moving out and getting ulcers.

What are you dragging ulcers in for? I said.

Take a ride in a NY taxi and see, he said. We have cabs no other city would allow in a amusement park for midgets. First, the doors barely open, so you have to turn sideways and try and get in. Then you bang your head against the top, which is made low for this purpose. You have to corkscrew in, thus spraining a mussel or your sacrediliac, and if it's raining or snow, you are in for a dandy surprise — because these taxis have a hump in the floor in back, and on each side of that hump is a 4 in. well like two dishpans. Each citizen brings in snow and rain, which drips down and fills up the dishpans, and since NY cabbies feel it against their relidgion

to ever clean out their cabs, which are moving garbage disposals, a very interesting collection of bilge floats in those dishpans. ...

... You can't sweep it out, on account of the dishpans being lower than the doors. You can't vacuum it out, it being mostly water. The only defense is this—(and now he hawls out a Carpenters Drill!) Make holes in the floor.

Water will certainly run right out of a hole, I decided.

Your mother would be proud of you at this moment, he said. And how about the Bus and Subway torture?

How's the Mayor suppose to even know what goes on in Buses or Subways? I said. He rides in a offishul limozine, with a driver to take him to and fro.

Then let's pass a law, he said, making the Mayor and all the politicians *ride in public transportation* for 1 week each year. Just 1 *week* of them dumbells waiting for Buses, getting hijacked into Subways, getting nauzeated from the stink of hotdogs and piazzas frying underground—just 1 week and Brother, you'd get some action!—Take Buses. Rush hour, they pass you in wolf packs, they're so full—while right across the street, going in the opp. direction, a fleet of empty Buses is racing to the Bronx, 10 miles away, *so's they can turn around!* Why can't every 2nd or 3rd empty turn around *right there*, instead of racing all the way up to the Bronx?

That would foul up their skedules, I said.

They are suppose to serve people, not skedules, he hollers. What about the holes in the streets?

With all this new bilding, they have to tear up the ground, I said.

They could put a limit on the number of holes, he said, like Mayor LaGardia used to. But not this Mayor, xcuse the xpression. He has raised the Art of making holes to new hights. He has xperts who do nothing but dig holes inside the holes already there. He has inspectors who, if there's a stretch of 3 blocks without a hole, the mistake is corrected before morning.

With so many holes, I am amazed you do not have to crawl to and fro, I said (but he don't even see I have throwed him a spitball).

I carry a board, he said. (You won't believe this, Mr. Mayor, but this kook is now showing me a Ironing Board!) This is part of the NYorker's Survival Kit, to get you across Bewildered Bob's trenches, foxholes, soors and open graves. He is changing NY from a Summer Festival to a All-Year Obstacle Race.

If you don't dig holes you don't get bildings, I defended.

Do you know what type monsterosities they now call bildings? he said.

Sure, I said. There's a new one right outside these windows.

That's why it's so nice and dark in your apt. all day, he said.

I'm not there much during the day, I said.

From the look of things you're not all there most of the time, he said. I will give you a refresher course on Wagner's Bilding Code, or How to Drive Americans Crazy in their Own Home. First, they make the ceilings so low you get an xtra floor every 4 floors — and that overloads all the elevators right there. Second, they make all the walls so thin no one will ever get lonesome. Everyone hears his neighbors gargling, taking a bath, or worse. In 1 new bilding, a tenant went to Florida leaving his TV on and it took the endgineers 2 days to figure out from which apt. the *Sunrise Semester* was coming to educate everyone at 6:30 A.M. ...

Let's get back to the traffick, I said coldly, which if you don't like you can always walk.

Walk? In NY? He laughed so hard you think he's watching Red Skeleton. You don't walk if you want to keep your love of animals. The Pidgeons flutter about your head and the dogs dirty your shoes. "Curb Your Dog" it says, but dogs don't read. ... What type earplugs do you use?

My ears do not hurt, I said.

You mean you sleep in NY without plugging your ears up? he xclaims. Even through this Croak of Doom horn the Fire Dept. shrewdly added to the heebie-jeebie sirens?

Which would you rather have, I said, people being woke up or the whole NY burning down?

Don't press me, he said. I'd burn ¾ of the new bildings with pleasure, starting with that Pam Am warehouse in the sky which will bring 25,000 more cattle to the worst crowded place they could find.

Mayor Wagner probably didn't even *know* the Pam Am bilding is going up there, I said.

That's true, he said.

I'm glad you give him 1 benefit of a dout, I said. . . .

Well, Mr. Mayor, what's the use? This screwball went on like that must of been 2 hours. By the time I manadge to get away, my mind is so xhausted from his Gasmask and Stickers and Rubber Hose and Ironing Board and Drill for draining out Taxis couldn't sleep a wink all night. That's when I heard the Croak of Doom horns. They were going like crazy.

Yours truly,
J. R. Jukes

QUESTIONS FOR DISCUSSION

1. How is the technical point of view in this letter like that in "I Can't Breathe"? How is it different?
2. Because Jukes repeats the remarks of a second person in his letter, what we have here is a reported dialogue within a monologue. Is this an advantage over a strict monologue? Why or why not? A character whose main purpose is to serve as a contrast for another, more central character is called a "foil." Which character is the foil here?
3. Point to examples of *hyperbole* in this letter.
4. Who or what is the object of Rosten's satire? Is he satirizing "the name" or "the vice"? What does Mayor Wagner have to do with this satire?

Understanding Words

An Interesting Word

You should know the history of the name "Jukes" to fully appreciate Rosten's use of it as a pseudonym. "Jukes" is the fictitious name of a New York family who, over several generations, displayed an abnormally high incidence of poverty, disease, stupidity, and criminal behavior. The case study has been challenged along with the methods of nineteenth-century sociologists, but the undesirable connotations of the name "Jukes" remain.

The Writer's Style

Burlesque is a form of satire in which there is an obvious discrepancy between the subject matter and the style in which the subject is treated. In burlesque, a serious subject is treated with ridicule, vulgarity, distortion, and often contempt. What is the usual style for a letter to a mayor or some other high official? Can you find evidence of burlesque in "An Open Letter to the Mayor of New York"?

Find examples of clichés, puns, and illiteracies in the letter. Is Rosten using irony here? Is either "speaker" in the letter aware of any irony in his words?

SUGGESTION FOR COMPOSITION

Write a satire in which you assume a false identity in order to satirize the sort of person you are pretending to be.

An Open Letter to the Mayor of New York

The following letter, which was actually sent to Representative Foreman, satirizes the federal government's farm subsidy program. The government has sometimes paid farmers for *not* producing goods, in order to prevent the drop in prices and the hardships to farmers that result from overproduction. J. B. Lee, Jr., "Potential Hog Raiser," opposes this procedure. But notice how he expresses his opposition.

Letter from a West Texas Constituent

J. B. Lee, Jr.

March 20, 1963

The Honorable Ed Foreman
House of Representatives
Congressional District #16
Washington 25, D.C.

Dear Sir:

My friend over in Terebone Parish received a $1,000 check from the government this year for not raising hogs. So I am going into the not-raising hog business next year.

What I want to know is, in your opinion, what is the best kind of farm to not raise hogs on and the best kind of hogs not to raise? I would prefer not to raise Razorbacks, but if that is not a good breed not to raise, I will just as gladly not raise any Berkshires or Durocs.

The hardest work in this business is going to be in keeping an inventory of how many hogs I haven't raised.

My friend is very joyful about the future of his business. He has been raising hogs for more than 20 years and the best he ever made was $400, until this year, when he got $1,000 for not raising hogs.

If I can get $1,000 for not raising 50 hogs, then will I get $2,000 for not raising 100 hogs? I plan to operate on a small scale at first, holding myself down to 4,000 hogs which means I will have $80,000 coming from the government.

Now, another thing: these hogs I will not raise will not eat 100,000 bushels of corn. So will you pay me anything for not raising 100,000 bushels of corn not to feed the hogs I am not raising?

I want to get started as soon as possible as this seems to be a good time of the year for not raising hogs.

One thing more, can I raise 10 or 12 hogs on the side while I am in the not-raising-hog-business just enough to get a few sides of bacon to eat?

Very truly yours,

J. B. Lee, Jr.
Potential Hog Raiser

JBL:gb

QUESTIONS FOR DISCUSSION

1. The first paragraph of Lee's letter is half truth and half fiction. Which is which? How do you know? Is the fiction any less reasonable than the truth?
2. A *paradox* is a statement or idea which seems self-contradictory or absurd but is somehow true. What paradox is central to Lee's letter?
3. Irony often involves the recognition of incongruities. Explain the irony in the idea that Mr. Lee's friend is earning $1,000 a year for not raising hogs. How much money did he earn for raising hogs? What is the relationship between paradox and irony? How do the simple style and rational tone of the letter contribute to the satire?
4. Compare and contrast J. B. Lee and J. R. Jukes. Which of them seems more aware of the incongruities of his remarks? In which letter is the writer's point of view closest to that of the author?

SUGGESTION FOR COMPOSITION

Write a letter in which you indirectly point out the absurdity of some custom or practice which annoys you. A school rule with which you do not agree might be a good subject, or some local, state, or national law. If you know quite a bit about international affairs, you can probably think of a subject in that area. The letter may be addressed to anyone — a friend or relative, the editor of a newspaper, a school official, or someone on the political scene. Be sure to state your complaints *indirectly*.

J. B. Lee's "Letter from a West Texas Constituent" is an example of the kind of satiric monologue in which the satirist wears an ironic mask. Lee assumed a certain role, pretending to be quite serious about an idea which was clearly absurd, in order to prove a point. Jonathan Swift did the same thing when he wrote "A Modest Proposal for Preventing the Children of Poor People in Ireland from Being a Burden to Their Parents or Country, and for Making Them Beneficial to the Public." Before you begin reading this masterpiece of satire, try to imagine Ireland in 1729.

The Satiric Voice

Swift's contemporaries included impoverished farmers, beggar women trying to keep their infants alive, tax collectors, and English landlords who collected rent from Irish property but lived abroad in order to avoid Irish taxes. When Swift wrote his article, other such pamphleteers had been drawn and quartered for speaking out against those in power. But it was no mere desire to hide that led Swift to employ the ironic mask.

A Modest Proposal

for Preventing the Children of Ireland from
Being a Burden to Their Parents or Country

Jonathan Swift

It is a melancholy object to those who walk through this great town or travel in the country, when they see the streets, the roads, and cabin doors crowded with beggars of the female sex, followed by three, four, or six children, all in rags, and importuning every passenger for an alms. These mothers, instead of being able to work for their honest livelihood, are forced to employ all their time in strolling to beg sustenance for their helpless infants, who, as they grow up, either turn thieves for want of work, or leave their dear native country, to fight for the Pretender in Spain, or sell themselves to the Barbadoes.

I think it is agreed by all parties, that this prodigious number of children in the arms, or on the backs, or at the heels of their mothers, and frequently of their fathers, is in the present deplorable state of the kingdom a very great additional grievance; and therefore whoever could find out a fair, cheap, and easy method of making these children sound and useful members of the commonwealth, would deserve so well of the public as to have his statue set up for a preserver of the nation.

But my intention is very far from being confined to provide only for the children of professed beggars; it is of a much greater extent, and shall take in the whole number of infants at a certain age, who are born of parents in effect as little able to support them, as those who demand our charity in the streets.

As to my own part, having turned my thoughts, for many years, upon this important subject, and maturely weighed the several schemes of other projectors, I have always found them grossly mistaken in their computation. It is true, a child just dropt from its dam, may be supported by her milk for a solar year with little other nourishment, at most not above the value of two shillings, which the mother may certainly get, or the value in scraps, by her lawful occupation of begging; and it is exactly at one year old that I propose to provide for them in such a manner, as, instead of being a charge upon their parents, or the parish, or wanting food and raiment for the rest of their lives, they shall, on the contrary, contribute to the feeding and partly to the clothing of many thousands.

There is likewise another great advantage in my scheme, that it will prevent those voluntary abortions, and that horrid practice of women murdering their illegitimate children, alas! too frequent among us—sacrificing the poor innocent babes, I doubt, more to avoid the expense than the shame—which would move tears and pity in the most savage and inhuman breast.

The number of souls in this kingdom being usually reckoned one million and a half, of these I calculate there may be about two hundred thousand couples whose wives are breeders; from which number I subtract thirty thousand couples, who are able to maintain their own children, although I apprehend there cannot be so many, under the present distresses of the kingdom; but this being granted, there will remain an hundred and seventy thousand breeders. I again subtract fifty thousand, for those women who miscarry, or whose children die by accident or disease within the year. There only remain an hundred and twenty thousand children of poor parents annually born: The question therefore is, How this number shall be reared, and provided for? which, as I have already said, under the present situation of affairs, is utterly impossible by all the methods hitherto proposed; for we can neither employ them in handicraft or agriculture; we neither build houses (I mean in the country), nor cultivate land: They can very seldom pick up a livelihood by stealing till they arrive at six years old, except where they are of towardly parts, although, I confess, they learn the rudiments much earlier; during which time they can however be properly looked upon only as probationers; as I have been informed by a principal gentleman in the county of Cavan, who protested to me, that he never knew above one or two instances under the age of six, even in a part of the kingdom so renowned for the quickest proficiency in that art.

I am assured by our merchants, that a boy or a girl before twelve years old, is no saleable commodity, and even when they come to this age, they will not yield above three pounds, or three pounds and half a crown at most, on the exchange; which cannot turn to account either to the parents or kingdom, the charge of nutriment and rags having been at least four times that value.

I shall now therefore humbly propose my own thoughts, which I hope will not be liable to the least objection.

I have been assured by a very knowing American of my acquaintance in London, that a young healthy child well nursed is at a year old a most delicious nourishing and wholesome food, whether stewed, roasted, baked, or boiled; and I make no doubt that it will equally serve in a fricassee, or a ragout.

I do therefore humbly offer it to public consideration, that of the hundred and twenty thousand children, already computed, twenty thousand may be reserved for breed, whereof only one fourth part to be males; which is more than we allow to sheep, black cattle, or swine; and my reason is that these children are seldom the fruits of marriage, a circumstance not much regarded by our savages; therefore one male will be sufficient to serve four females. That the remaining hundred thousand may, at a year old, be offered in the sale to the persons of quality and fortune through the kingdom; always advising the mother to let them suck plentifully in the last month, so as to render them plump and fat for a good table. A child will make two dishes at an entertainment for friends; and when the family dines alone, the fore or hind quarter will make a reasonable dish, and seasoned with a little pepper or salt will be very good boiled on the fourth day, especially in winter.

I have reckoned upon a medium that a child just born will weigh twelve pounds, and in a solar year, if tolerably nursed, increaseth to twenty-eight pounds.

I grant this food will be somewhat dear, and therefore very proper for landlords, who, as they have already devoured most of the parents, seem to have the best title to the children.

Infants' flesh will be in season throughout the year, but more plentiful in March, and a little before and after; for we are told by a grave author, an eminent French physician, that fish being a prolific diet, there are more children born in Roman Catholic countries about nine months after Lent than at any other season; therefore, reckoning a year after Lent, the markets will be more glutted than usual, because the number of popish infants is at least three to one in this kingdom: and therefore it will have one other collateral advantage, by lessening the number of papists among us.

I have already computed the charge of nursing a beggar's child (in which list I reckon all cottagers, laborers, and four fifths of the farmers) to be about two shillings per annum, rags included; and I believe no gentleman would repine to give ten shillings for the carcass of a good fat child, which, as I have said, will make four dishes of excellent nutritive meat, when he hath only some particular friend or his own family to dine with him. Thus the squire will learn to be a good landlord, and grow popular among his tenants; the mother will have eight shillings net profit, and be fit for work till she produces another child.

Those who are more thrifty (as I must confess the times require) may flay the carcass, the skin of which artificially dressed will make admirable gloves for ladies, and summer boots for fine gentlemen.

As to our city of Dublin, shambles may be appointed for this purpose in the most convenient parts of it, and butchers we may be assured will not be wanting; although I rather recommend buying the children alive and dressing them hot from the knife, as we do roasting pigs.

A very worthy person, a true lover of his country, and whose virtues I highly esteem, was lately pleased in discoursing on this matter to offer a refinement upon my scheme. He said that many gentlemen of this kingdom, having of late destroyed their deer, he conceived that the want of venison might be well supplied by the bodies of young lads and maidens, not exceeding fourteen years of age nor under twelve; so great a number of both sexes in every country being now ready to starve for want of work and service; and these to be disposed of by their parents if alive, or otherwise by their nearest relations. But with due deference to so excellent a friend, and so deserving a patriot, I cannot be altogether in his sentiments; for as to the males, my American acquaintance assured me from frequent experience, that their flesh was generally tough and lean, like that of our schoolboys, by continual exercise, and their taste disagreeable, and to fatten them would not answer the charge. Then as to the females, it would, I think with humble submission, be a loss to the public, because they soon would become breeders themselves: And besides it is not improbable that some scrupulous people might be apt to censure such a practice (although indeed very unjustly) as a little bordering upon cruelty, which, I confess, hath always been with me the strongest objection against any project, how well soever intended.

But in order to justify my friend, he confessed, that this expedient was put into his head by the famous Psalmanazar, a native of the island Formosa, who came from thence to London, above twenty years ago, and in conversation told my friend, that in his country when any young person happened to be put to death, the executioner sold the carcass to persons of quality, as a prime dainty, and that, in his time, the body of a plump girl of fifteen, who was crucified for an attempt to poison the Emperor, was sold to his Imperial Majesty's prime minister of state, and other great mandarins of the court, in joints from the gibbet, at four hundred crowns. Neither indeed can I deny, that if the same use were made of several plump young girls in this town, who, without one single groat to their fortunes, cannot stir abroad without a chair, and appear at a playhouse and assemblies in foreign fineries which they never will pay for, the kingdom would not be the worse.

Some persons of a desponding spirit are in great concern about that vast number of poor people, who are aged, diseased, or maimed, and I have been desired to employ my thoughts what course may be taken, to ease the nation of so grievous an encumbrance. But I am not in the least pain upon that matter, because it is very well known, that they are every day dying, and rotting, by cold, and famine, and filth, and vermin, as fast as can be reasonably expected. And as to the younger laborers, they are now in almost as hopeful a condition. They cannot get work, and consequently pine away for want of nourishment, to a degree, that if at any time they are accidentally hired to common labour, they have not strength to perform it, and thus the country and themselves are happily delivered from the evils to come.

I have too long digressed, and therefore shall return to my subject. I think the advantages by the proposal which I have made are obvious and many, as well as of the highest importance.

For *first*, as I have already observed, it would greatly lessen the number of papists, with whom we are yearly overrun, being the principal breeders of the nation, as well as our most dangerous enemies, and who stay at home on purpose with a design to deliver the kingdom to the Pretender, hoping to take their advantage by the absence of so many good Protestants, who have chosen rather to leave their country, than stay at home, and pay tithes against their conscience to an Episcopal curate.

Secondly, the poorer tenants will have something valuable of their own, which by law may be made liable to distress and help to pay their landlord's rent, their corn and cattle being already seized, and money a thing unknown.

Thirdly, whereas the maintenance of an hundred thousand children, from two years old and upward, cannot be computed at less than ten

A Modest Proposal

33

shillings apiece per annum, the nation's stock will be thereby increased fifty thousand pounds per annum, besides the profit of a new dish introduced to the tables of all gentlemen of fortune in the kingdom who have any refinement in taste. And the money will circulate among ourselves, the goods being entirely of our own growth and manufacture.

Fourthly, the constant breeders, beside the gain of eight shillings sterling per annum by the sale of their children, will be rid of the charge of maintaining them after the first year.

Fifthly, this food would likewise bring great custom to taverns, where the vintners will certainly be so prudent as to procure the best receipts for dressing it to perfection, and consequently have their houses frequented by all the fine gentlemen who justly value themselves upon their knowledge in good eating; and a skillful cook, who understands how to oblige his guests, will contrive to make it as expensive as they please.

Sixthly, this would be a great inducement to marriage, which all wise nations have either encouraged by rewards or enforced by laws and penalties. It would increase the care and the tenderness of mothers toward their children, when they were sure of a settlement for life to the poor babes, provided in some sort by the public, to their annual profit instead of expense. We should soon see an honest emulation among the married women, which of them could bring the fattest child to the market. Men would become as fond of their wives during the time of their pregnancy as they are now of their mares in foal, their cows in calf, their sows when they are ready to farrow; nor offer to beat or kick them (as is too frequent a practice) for fear of a miscarriage.

Many other advantages might be enumerated. For instance, the addition of some thousand carcasses in our exportation of barreled beef, the propagation of swine's flesh, and improvement in the art of making good bacon, so much wanted among us by the great destruction of pigs, too frequent at our tables; which are no way comparable in taste or magnificence to a well-grown, fat, yearling child, which roasted whole will make a considerable figure at a lord mayor's feast or any other public entertainment. But this and many others I omit, being studious of brevity.

Supposing that one thousand families in this city would be constant customers for infants' flesh, besides others who might have it at merry meetings, particularly at weddings and christenings, I compute that Dublin would take off annually about twenty thousand carcasses; and the rest of the kingdom (where probably they will be sold somewhat cheaper) the remaining eighty thousand.

I can think of no one objection that will possibly be raised against this proposal, unless it should be urged that the number of people will be thereby much lessened in the kingdom. This I freely own, and 'twas indeed one principal design in offering it to the world. I desire the reader will observe that I calculate my remedy for this one individual kingdom of Ireland, and for no other that ever was, is, or, I think, ever can be upon earth. Therefore let no man talk to me of other expedients: of taxing our absentees at five shillings a pound: of using neither clothes, nor household furniture, except what is of our own growth and manufacture: of utterly rejecting the materials and instruments that promote foreign luxury: of curing the expensiveness of pride, vanity, idleness, and gaming in our women: of introducing a vein of parsimony, prudence and temperance: of learning to love our country, wherein we differ even from Laplanders, and the inhabitants of Topinamboo: of quitting our animosities, and factions, nor act any longer like the ~~Jews~~, who were murdering one another at the very moment their city was taken: of being a little cautious not to sell our country and consciences for nothing: of teaching landlords to have at least one degree of mercy towards their tenants. Lastly, of putting a spirit of honesty, industry, and skill into our shopkeepers, who, if a resolution could now be taken to buy only our native goods, would immediately unite to cheat and exact upon us in the price, the measure, and the goodness, nor could ever yet be brought to make one fair proposal of just dealing, though often and earnestly invited to it.

Therefore I repeat, let no man talk to me of these and the like expedients, till he hath at least some glimpse of hope, that there will ever be some hearty and sincere attempt to put them in practice.

But as to my self, having been wearied out for many years with offering vain, idle, visionary thoughts, and at length utterly despairing of success, I fortunately fell upon this proposal, which as it is wholly new, so it hath something solid and real, of no expense and little trouble, full in our own power, and whereby we can incur no danger in disobliging England. For this kind of commodity will not bear exportation, the flesh being of too tender a consistence, to admit a long continuance in salt, although perhaps I could name a country, which would be glad to eat up our whole nation without it.

After all, I am not so violently bent upon my own opinion, as to reject any offer, proposed by wise men, which shall be found equally innocent, cheap, easy, and effectual. But before something of that kind shall be advanced in contradiction to my scheme, and offering a better, I desire

A Modest Proposal

the author or authors, will be pleased maturely to consider two points. *First*, as things now stand, how they will be able to find food and raiment for a hundred thousand useless mouths and backs. And *secondly*, there being a round million of creatures in human figure throughout this kingdom, whose whole subsistence put into a common stock would leave them in debt two millions of pounds sterling, adding those who are beggars by profession, to the bulk of farmers, cottagers and labourers, with their wives and children, who are beggars in effect; I desire those politicians, who dislike my overture, and may perhaps be so bold to attempt an answer, that they will first ask the parents of these mortals, whether they would not at this day think it a great happiness to have been sold for food at a year old, in the manner I prescribe, and thereby have avoided such a perpetual scene of misfortunes as they have since gone through, by the oppression of landlords, the impossibility of paying rent without money or trade, the want of common sustenance, with neither house nor clothes to cover them from the inclemencies of the weather, and the most inevitable prospect of entailing the like or greater miseries upon their breed for ever.

I profess, in the sincerity of my heart, that I have not the least personal interest in endeavoring to promote this necessary work, having no other motive than the public good of my country, by advancing our trade, providing for infants, relieving the poor, and giving some pleasure to the rich. I have no children by which I can propose to get a single penny; the youngest being nine years old, and my wife past childbearing.

QUESTIONS FOR DISCUSSION

1. Make a list of the arguments Swift uses to present his case. Then answer or "translate" each argument in terms of Swift's real feelings.
2. Which kind of satire is "A Modest Proposal," Juvenalian or Horatian?
3. Describe the speaker's tone in "A Modest Proposal." Is it emotional, or does it seem cool and logical? How does this tone contribute to the satire?

4. Are we given any real facts in the article? What are they? What do they prove?

5. At one point, the speaker says that the aged poor "are every day dying, and rotting, by cold, and famine, and filth, and vermin, as fast as can be reasonably expected. And as to the younger labourers, they are now in almost as hopeful a condition." Which specific words and phrases in this passage reveal Swift's irony?

6. In order to alert people to the truth of a matter, a satirist sometimes uses repugnant or shocking language and images. How does Swift use shock in this article?

7. From your answers to the preceding questions, formulate a description of Swift's irony. Include in your description some mention of his main idea.

8. Is the speaker in "A Modest Proposal" Swift himself? How does the speaker's point of view differ from Swift's point of view? What are Swift's purposes in adopting a mask? Does the mask strengthen the force of his argument? Does it prevent the reader from accusing Swift of prejudice? Why is the mask a good vehicle for irony?

9. Even when he pretends to reject them, Swift advocates specific practical measures to alleviate the social and economic problems of Ireland in his time. What specific measures does he advocate?

Understanding Words

The Writer's Style

The sting of Swift's satire arises from the vast disparity between the humble manner of the speaker and the substance of his proposal. Consider these phrases from the first two paragraphs: *melancholy object, forced to employ all their time in strolling to beg sustenance, dear native country, prodigious number, deplorable state of the kingdom, additional grievance, preserver of the nation.* How do they influence your initial response to the speaker? Once you know the proposal, does your attitude toward the speaker change? Does the speaker's language change? Point to specific words which show that the speaker is using the language of the wealthy mercantilist who believes that trade among nations is more important to a country than the individuals who live there.

A Modest Proposal

When you read "A Modest Proposal," you may have found the subject too remote from your own time and experience to affect you very strongly. The following satire was written in 1956 by Harry Golden, who uses an approach very similar to Swift's as he asks you to take a look at *your* world.

The Vertical Negro Plan

Harry Golden

Those who love North Carolina will jump at the chance to share in the great responsibility confronting our Governor and the State Legislature. A special session of the Legislature (July 25 — 28, 1956) passed a series of amendments to the State Constitution. These proposals submitted by the Governor and his Advisory Education Committee included the following:

(A) The elimination of the compulsory attendance law, "to prevent any child from being forced to attend a school with a child of another race."
(B) The establishment of "Education Expense Grants" for education in a private school, "in the case of a child assigned to a public school attended by a child of another race."
(C) A "uniform system of local option" whereby a majority of the folks in a school district may suspend or close a school if the situation becomes "intolerable."

But suppose a Negro child applies for this "Education Expense Grant" and says he wants to go to the private school too? There are fourteen Supreme Court decisions involving the use of public funds; there are only two "decisions" involving the elimination of racial discrimination in the public schools.

The Governor has said that critics of these proposals have not offered any constructive advice or alternatives. Permit me, therefore, to offer an idea for the consideration of the members of the regular sessions. A careful study of my plan, I believe, will show that it will save millions of dollars in tax funds and eliminate forever the danger to our public education system. Before I outline my plan, I would like to give you a little background.

One of the factors involved in our tremendous industrial growth and economic prosperity is the fact that the South, voluntarily, has all but eliminated VERTICAL SEGREGATION. The tremendous buying power of the twelve million Negroes in the South has been based wholly on the absence of racial segregation. The white and Negro stand at the same grocery and supermarket counters; deposit money at the same bank teller's window; pay phone and light bills to the same clerk; walk through the same dime and department stores, and stand at the same drugstore counters.

It is only when the Negro "sets" that the fur begins to fly.

Now, since we are not even thinking about restoring VERTICAL SEGREGATION, I think my plan would not only comply with the Supreme Court decisions, but would maintain "sitting-down" segregation. Now here is the GOLDEN VERTICAL NEGRO PLAN. Instead of all those complicated proposals, all the next session needs to do is pass one small amendment which would provide *only* desks in all the public schools of our state—*no seats.*

The Vertical Negro Plan

39

The desks should be those standing-up jobs, like the old-fashioned bookkeeping desk. Since no one in the South pays the slightest attention to a VERTICAL NEGRO, this will completely solve our problem. And it is not such a terrible inconvenience for young people to stand up during their classroom studies. In fact, this may be a blessing in disguise. They are not learning to read sitting down, anyway; maybe standing up will help. This will save more millions of dollars in the cost of our remedial English course when the kids enter college. In whatever direction you look, with the GOLDEN VERTICAL NEGRO PLAN you save millions of dollars, to say nothing of eliminating forever any danger to our public education system upon which rests the destiny, hopes, and happiness of this society.

My WHITE BABY PLAN offers another possible solution to the segregation problem—this time in a field other than education.

Here is an actual case history of the "White Baby Plan to End Racial Segregation":

Some months ago there was a revival of the Laurence Olivier movie, *Hamlet,* and several Negro schoolteachers were eager to see it. One Saturday afternoon they asked some white friends to lend them two of their little children, a three-year-old girl and a six-year-old boy, and, holding these white children by the hands, they obtained tickets from the movie-house cashier without a moment's hesitation. They were in like Flynn.

This would also solve the baby-sitting problem for thousands and thousands of white working mothers. There can be a mutual exchange of references, then the people can sort of pool their children at a central point in each neighborhood, and every time a Negro wants to go to the movies all she need do is pick up a white child—and go.

Eventually the Negro community can set up a factory and manufacture white babies made of plastic, and when they want to go to the opera or to a concert, all they need do is carry that plastic doll in their arms. The dolls, of course, should all have blond curls and blue eyes, which would go even further; it would give the Negro woman and her husband priority over the whites for the very best seats in the house.

While I still have faith in the WHITE BABY PLAN, my final proposal may prove to be the most practical of all.

Only after a successful test was I ready to announce formally the GOLDEN "OUT-OF-ORDER" PLAN.

I tried my plan in a city of North Carolina, where the Negroes represent 39 percent of the population.

I prevailed upon the manager of a department store to shut the water off in his "white" water fountain and put up a sign, "Out-of-Order." For the first day or two the whites were hesitant, but little by little they began to drink out of the water fountain belonging to the "coloreds"— and by the end of the third week everybody was drinking the "segregated" water; with not a single solitary complaint to date.

I believe the test is of such sociological significance that the Governor should appoint a special committee of two members of the House and two Senators to investigate the GOLDEN "OUT-OF-ORDER" PLAN. We kept daily reports on the use of the unsegregated water fountain which should be of great value to this committee. This may be the answer to the necessary uplifting of the white morale. It is possible that the whites may accept desegregation if they are assured that the facilities are still "separate," albeit "Out-of-Order."

As I see it now, the key to my Plan is to keep the "Out-of-Order" sign up for at least two years. We must do this thing gradually.

QUESTIONS FOR DISCUSSION

1. Why does Golden begin his article with a reference to "those who love North Carolina"? What is the "great responsibility"?
2. Explain the three amendments to the State Constitution.
3. What is the significance of the fact that there were fourteen Supreme Court decisions related to the use of public funds and only two "decisions" specifically related to the elimination of racial discrimination?
4. What does Golden offer his reader in order to persuade him to listen to his plan — that is, what material advantage does he say his plan will have?
5. Explain what Golden means by "vertical segregation."
6. Golden says, "The tremendous buying power of the twelve million Negroes in the South has been based wholly on the absence of racial segregation." Does he mean what he says, or is he being ironic? What

The Vertical Negro Plan

does his statement tell you about segregation, integration, and the economy?

7. Golden pursues his argument that "vertical" integration is an accomplished fact to its "logical conclusion": Negroes would be allowed in "white" schools if they did not sit down. How reasonable is this argument? Is *paradox* involved here? Explain.

8. How does he comment on the quality of education in the public schools of North Carolina?

9. Explain the "White Baby Plan." Why would the white, plastic baby dolls have blue eyes and blonde curls? What does the "White Baby Plan" tell you about the terms on which whites, according to Golden, would accept Negroes in places of public entertainment?

10. Explain the irony of the "Out-of-Order" plan. Which sentence in the essay best sums up this irony?

11. Why does Golden say, "This may be the answer to the necessary uplifting of the white morale"?

12. Does Golden really believe that his three plans would accomplish desegregation while keeping all parties happy? Is he writing this essay in order to propose what he believes to be reasonable steps to accomplish desegregation, or is he writing in order to say something about things as they are?

Understanding Words

The Writer's Style

Golden combines slang and formal language in this essay, as he did in "Let's Take Bubble Gum Out of the Schools." Compare the phrases "jump at the chance" and "great responsibility confronting" in the first sentence. Why is the combination of these two levels of usage effective at the beginning of an essay? How does it establish the tone for this particular essay?

SUGGESTIONS FOR COMPOSITION

1. Write a short essay discussing the similarities between "A Modest Proposal" and "The Vertical Negro Plan." Pay particular attention to the authors' use of irony and facts.

2. Using any form you wish—letter, essay, editorial—write a satire in which you adopt an ironic mask.

PARODIES

You have seen caricatures—cartoons in which familiar faces are drawn with their prominent features exaggerated and distorted. Although the drawings are not realistic, they are comically like their models. Writers sometimes produce "caricatures" of familiar pieces of literature. They alter the details in a humorous way but retain enough of the style, structure, and subject of the original so that a reader who knows the original will recognize it. This sort of imitation is a form of satire called *parody*. (It should not be confused with *plagiarism*.)

A parody usually resembles its model in form and technical point of view. That is, if the original is a poem, the parody will be a poem; if the original is a monologue, the parody will usually be a monologue. The concrete subject will be similar, too; and the characters, though they will be distorted to some degree, will closely resemble those in the original work. The main differences will be seen in the details of style, characterization, dialogue, description. The satirist's alterations reveal his attitude toward the original. The humor of parody, then, lies in the comparison of the original and the imitation.

"*Surely, Son, you can find something to paint indoors.*"

Drawing by Kovarsky; © 1957 The New Yorker Magazine, Inc.

You may have read *Alice in Wonderland* or *Through the Looking Glass,* but you may not have realized that much of Lewis Carroll's verse is parody. His nonsense verse is amusing enough to have outlasted most of the works he imitated. Many children in Carroll's time could recognize his allusions to the stuffy, moral verses which instructed them how to behave like little ladies and gentlemen. One of the following two poems was written by Robert Southey; the other is Carroll's parody. Which is which? How can you tell?

1

"You are old, Father William," the young man cried;
    "The few locks which are left you are gray;
You are hale, Father William—a hearty old man:
    Now tell me the reason, I pray."

"In the days of my youth," Father William replied,   5
    "I remembered that youth would fly fast,
And abused not my health and my vigor at first,
    That I never might need them at last."

"You are old, Father William," the young man cried,
    "And pleasures with youth pass away;   10
And yet you lament not the days that are gone:
    Now tell me the reason, I pray."

"In the days of my youth," Father William replied,
    "I remembered that youth could not last;
I thought of the future, whatever I did,   15
    That I never might grieve for the past."

"You are old, Father William," the young man cried,
    "And life must be hastening away;
You are cheerful and love to converse upon death:
    Now tell me the reason, I pray."   20

"I am cheerful, young man," Father William replied;
    "Let the cause thy attention engage;
In the days of my youth, I remembered my God,
    And He hath not forgotten my age."

2

"You are old, Father William," the young man said,
    "And your hair has become very white;
And yet you incessantly stand on your head—
    Do you think, at your age, it is right?"

"In my youth," Father William replied to his son,   5
    "I feared it might injure the brain;
But now that I'm perfectly sure I have none,
    Why, I do it again and again."

"You are old," said the youth, "as I mentioned before,
    And have grown most uncommonly fat;   10
Yet you turned a back-somersault in at the door—
    Pray, what is the reason for that?"

"In my youth," said the sage, as he shook his grey locks,
    "I kept all my limbs very supple
By the use of this ointment—one shilling the box—   15
    Allow me to sell you a couple."

"You are old," said the youth, "and your jaws are too weak
    For anything tougher than suet;
Yet you finished the goose, with the bones and the beak—
    Pray how did you manage to do it?"   20

"In my youth," said his father, "I took to the law,
    And argued each case with my wife;
And the muscular strength, which it gave to my jaw,
    Has lasted the rest of my life."

"You are old," said the youth, "one would hardly suppose   25
    That your eye was as steady as ever;
Yet you balanced an eel on the end of your nose—
    What made you so awfully clever?"

"I have answered three questions, and that is enough,"
    Said his father; "don't give yourself airs!   30
Do you think I can listen all day to such stuff?
    Be off, or I'll kick you downstairs!"

You Are Old,
Father William

1. Is the second poem a parody of style, a parody of content, or both? Compare the style of the two poems.
2. Which "Father William" do you like the best? Does one seem more foolish than the other? Do you think that "age" likes to give this kind of advice to "youth"? What does Lewis Carroll think of Father William and of the young man looking for advice? How can you tell what Carroll thinks?
3. When a satirist writes a parody, he is likely to adjust the style of the original in some way. He may assume a *mock-serious* tone, pretending to take seriously a subject which he actually views as absurd. Or he may use *burlesque* humor, treating a basically serious subject in a casual, absurd, earthy, perhaps even vulgar manner. In either case, the effect of the original is drastically changed. Which of these approaches best describes Lewis Carroll's treatment of Robert Southey's poem?

In addition to satirizing the pretentious pose of an old man delivering advice to a young one, Carroll was satirizing a shallow, artificial poem that expressed tiresome thoughts. As you read the following poems and parodies, try to determine whether Ogden Nash is satirizing the original poems themselves or something else which the poems merely represent.

The Passionate Shepherd to His Love

Christopher Marlowe

Come live with me and be my love,
And we will all the pleasures prove
That valleys, groves, hills, and fields,
Woods, or steepy mountain yields.

And we will sit upon the rocks,
Seeing the shepherds feed their flocks,
By shallow rivers to whose falls
Melodious birds sing madrigals.

5

And I will make thee beds of roses
And a thousand fragrant posies,   10
A cap of flowers, and a kirtle
Embroidered all with leaves of myrtle;

A gown made of the finest wool
Which from our pretty lambs we pull;
Fair lined slippers for the cold,   15
With buckles of the purest gold;

A belt of straw and ivy buds,
With coral clasps and amber studs:
And if these pleasures may thee move,
Come live with me, and be my love.   20

The shepherds' swains shall dance and sing
For thy delight each May morning:
If these delights thy mind may move,
Then live with me and be my love.

Love Under the Republicans
(or Democrats)

Ogden Nash

Come live with me and be my love
And we will all the pleasures prove
Of a marriage conducted with economy
In the Twentieth Century Anno Donomy.
We'll live in a dear little walk-up flat   5
With practically room to swing a cat
And a potted cactus to give it hauteur
And a bathtub equipped with dark brown water.
We'll eat, without undue discouragement
Foods low in cost but high in nouragement   10
And quaff with pleasure, while chatting wittily,
The peculiar wine of Little Italy.
We'll remind each other it's smart to be thrifty
And buy our clothes for something-fifty.
We'll stand in line on holidays   15
For seats at unpopular matinees,
And every Sunday we'll have a lark
And take a walk in Central Park.
And one of these days not too remote
I'll probably up and cut your throat.   20

1. Is Nash's imitation of Marlowe's style exact? Explain.
2. Compare the content of the two poems. Which speaker offers his love the more romantic inducements? Which one is more realistic? Do Marlowe's sentiments become absurd in "The Twentieth Century Anno Donomy"? What sort of promises does a girl expect from her suitor these days, "beds of roses" or "a dear little walk-up flat"?
3. Why does the speaker in the Nash poem say "I'll probably up and cut your throat"?
4. In your own words, state the thought expressed in the Nash satire. What is the object of his satire—Marlowe, romantic love, modernity, the Republicans (or Democrats), romantic poetry?
5. Why does Nash mention the two political parties in his title?
6. Does burlesque humor operate in this parody? Explain.

Abou Ben Adhem

Leigh Hunt

Abou Ben Adhem (may his tribe increase!)
Awoke one night from a deep dream of peace,
And saw, within the moonlight in his room,
Making it rich, and like a lily in bloom,
An angel writing in a book of gold:—   5
Exceeding peace had made Ben Adhem bold,
And to the presence in the room he said,
"What writest thou?"—The vision raised its head,
And with a look made of all sweet accord,
Answered, "The names of those who love the Lord."   10
"And is mine one?" said Abou. "Nay, not so,"
Replied the angel. Abou spoke more low,
But cheerly still; and said, "I pray thee, then,
Write me as one that loves his fellow-men."
The angel wrote, and vanished. The next night   15
It came again with a great wakening light,
And showed the names whom love of God had blessed,
And lo! Ben Adhem's name led all the rest.

A Bas Ben Adhem

Ogden Nash

My fellow man I do not care for.
I often ask me, What's he there for?
The only answer I can find
Is, Reproduction of his kind.
If I'm supposed to swallow that,   5
Winnetka is my habitat.
Isn't it time to carve Hic Jacet
Above that Reproduction racket?

To make the matter more succinct:
Suppose my fellow man extinct.   10
Why, who would not approve the plan
Save possibly my fellow man?
Yet with a politician's voice
He names himself as Nature's choice.

The finest of the human race   15
Are bad in figure, worse in face.
Yet just because they have two legs
And come from storks instead of eggs
They count the spacious firmament
As something to be charged and sent.

Paul Klee

Though man created smocks and snoods
And one-way streets and breakfast foods,
And double features and mustard plasters,
And Huey Longs and Lady Astors,
He hails himself with drum and fife   25
And bullies lower forms of life.

Not that I think that much depends
On how we treat our feathered friends,
Or claim the wart hog in the zoo
Is nearer God than me or you;   30
Just that I wonder, as I scan,
The wherefore of my fellow man.

QUESTIONS FOR DISCUSSION

1. In Leigh Hunt's poem, "Ben Adhem's name led all the rest." Why? State the central idea of Hunt's poem in a single sentence.
2. What is the central idea of Nash's poem? Does Nash agree with Hunt? Does Nash believe that man is the finest object of man's esteem?
3. How does Nash use rhyme to emphasize humor in his verse?
4. As cited by Nash, are the accomplishments of man noble or wonderful?
5. What is the general tone of the satire in "A Bas Ben Adhem"? Is there truth in what Nash says, or is he simply writing to entertain? Compare the picture of humanity in this poem to that in Swift's "A Modest Proposal."
6. What is the significance of Nash's title, "A *Bas* Ben Adhem"?
7. Certain situations are repeatedly used by comics to get a laugh: the elegant lady who falls on her face; the calm, rational man who suddenly explodes; the little old lady who smokes cigars in private; the oddly matched couple; the wedding that turns into a brawl. Point to examples of unexpected contrasts and incongruities in the parodies you have read, and explain how they are used satirically. Look particularly for examples of lofty language used in an absurd way, sentimental or serious subjects treated in a burlesque manner, and trivial subjects treated in a mock-serious manner.

Before you read the essay, consider these lines from the philosopher Bertrand Russell. Updike probably had much the same thing in mind when he wrote his parody.

Be very wary of opinions that flatter your self-esteem. Both men and women, nine times out of ten, are firmly convinced of the superior excellence of their own sex. There is abundant evidence on both sides. If you are a man, you can point out that most poets and men of science are male; if you are a woman, you can retort that so are most criminals.

The American Man: What of *Him*?

(An Editorial Left Out of *Life's* Special 35¢ Issue: "The American Woman")

John Updike

Ever since the history-dimmed day when Christopher Columbus, a Genoese male, turned his three ships (*Niña, Pinta, Santa María*) toward the United States, men have also played a significant part in the development of our nation. Lord Baltimore, who founded the colony of Maryland for Roman Catholics driven by political persecution from Europe's centuries-old shores, was a man. So was Wyatt Earp, who brought Anglo-Saxon common law into a vast area then in the grip of a *potpourri* of retributive justice, "vigilantism," and the ancient Code Napoléon. Calvin Coolidge, the thirtieth Chief Executive, was male. The list could be extended indefinitely.

Things were not always easy for the American Man. He came here in his water-weathered ships and did not find broad thruways, "cloud-capped towers," and a ready-made Free Way of Life. No, what he found confronting him in this fabled New Land was, principally, trees. Virgin, deciduous, hundreds of feet taller than he, the trees of the Colonization left their scars on his mental makeup in the form of the high rates of alcoholism, suicide, and divorce that distinguish him from the men of Continental Europe or Australasia. While his brethren of the Old World were dandling perfumed coquettes on their silk-garbed knees, he was forging inward, across the Appalachians to the Great Prairie, where his woods-tested faith, tempered in the forge of Valley Forge and honed on the heights of Mont-

calm's Quebec, took on a new austerity and became Evangelical Methodism. The Chevaliers of France didn't give him pause, nor the wetbacks of Mexico. But he did not emerge on the spray-moistened cliffs of California the same man who sailed from Southampton, Brussels, or Rügen. As Robert Frost says, in his quietly affirmative lines:

> The land was ours before we were the land's. . . .
> Possessing what we still were unpossessed by,
> Possessed by what we now no more possessed.

What is it that distinguishes the American Man from his counterparts in other climes; what *is* it that makes him so special? He is religious. He is quietly affirmative. He is trustworthy, loyal, helpful, friendly, courteous, kind, obedient, cheerful, thrifty, brave, clean, and reverent. He carries his burdens lightly, his blessings responsibly. Unlike the Oriental mandarin, he shaves his upper lip. Nor does he let his fingernails grow. Unlike the men of England, he does not wear gloves. Generally, he is taller than the men of nations (e.g., Nepal, Switzerland) where the average height is, compared to ours, laughable. All over the world, coolies and fakirs are picking themselves up out of the age-old mire and asking, "How can we become like Yanqui men?" Our State Department, cleansed of intellectual southpaws, works night and day on the answer.

The American Man has his faults, too. He loves speed. Is speed, in every case, desirable, per se? The editors, no strangers to speed themselves, wonder, for "the race is not [always] to the swift, nor the battle to the strong." The American Man tends to swagger—understandably. He enjoys bowling. He spends more money on bowling each year than the entire income of the Grand Duchy of Luxembourg since the Hapsburgs. Our critics in India, perhaps with justice, lift their eyebrows at this. But he is big, *big*—a big man—and he does things in a big way. He smokes too much and laughs too hard. The popcorn alone that he devours every year would outweigh Mont Blanc. He has more insidious shortcomings, too, but space limitations preclude our listing them.

He can look back over a hundred and eighty years of steady betterment with forward-looking pride. Today, men are active in every walk of LIFE. Politics: Several of our ablest senators are male, and men like John Foster Dulles, Charles Wilson, and Dwight David Eisenhower figure prominently in Washington's innermost councils. Religion: Reinhold Niebuhr has just this year delivered a sermon. Industry: Men are infiltrating the top levels of management, and already dominate such diverse fields as structural engineering, anthracite development, track and field events, and fire control. The Arts: Individual men like Herman Wouk and Archibald MacLeish have authored works in every way comparable to the best of Willa Cather or Mary Roberts Rinehart, the Queen of American Mystery Fiction.

The American Man can be proud of his sex. In the home, though still docile, he cunningly gets his way. In the community, he is a model for all young boys, as to what manhood means. In the state, he pays income tax or sales tax, depending. In the nation, he makes up only slightly less than half the population. Perhaps most importantly, he has solved the millennia-old riddle of the sage:

What is Man, that Thou art mindful of him?

QUESTIONS FOR DISCUSSION

1. In his first sentence, Updike says that "men have also played a significant part in the development of our nation." What is the effect of his use of the word "also"? Later, Updike says, "The list could be extended indefinitely." You have seen how satirists use *hyperbole*, or extravagant exaggeration. The opposite of this, *understatement*, is another useful satirical device. Which device is Updike using in the above examples?
2. Is the tone of Updike's essay logical, scientific, factual? For instance, is he being serious in the second paragraph where he describes the psychological effect of trees on the first colonists of North America?
3. Does Updike view the American Man as a "boy scout"? Does he see him as a hero? Is it true that men of older civilizations all over the world are asking themselves how they can become more like American men?
4. How admirable are the characteristics of the American Man that Updike describes in paragraph four? Compare Updike here to Nash in "A Bas Ben Adhem." What is Updike suggesting about similar articles on the American Woman?
5. Describe Updike's tone in each of the following statements. Can you say what he is satirizing in each case?
   a) "Calvin Coolidge, the thirtieth Chief Executive, was male."
   b) "He came here in his water-weathered ships and did not find broad thruways, 'cloud-capped towers,' and a ready-made Free Way of Life."

c) "Unlike the Oriental mandarin, he shaves his upper lip. Nor does he let his fingernails grow."

d) "... where the average height is, compared to ours, laughable."

e) "He can look back over a hundred and eighty years of steady betterment with forward-looking pride."

f) "The Arts: Individual men like Herman Wouk and Archibald MacLeish have authored works in every way comparable to the best of Willa Cather or Mary Roberts Rinehart, the Queen of American Mystery Fiction."

g) "In the home, though still docile, he cunningly gets his way."

h) "Perhaps most importantly, he has solved the millennia-old riddle of the sage: ..."

i) "Our State Department, cleansed of intellectual southpaws ..."

6. What, do you think, were Updike's motives for writing this essay?

7. What attitude does Updike seem to have toward *Life* magazine?

SUGGESTIONS FOR COMPOSITION

1. Find an example of highly sentimental or didactic verse and write a parody of it, imitating both the style and the content.

2. Write a parody of some particular kind of writing that most of the people in your class will recognize. Or, write a speech which satirizes a certain style with which your class will be familiar. Plan to present the speech to the class.

SATIRIC NARRATIVES

You will find that the voice of the satirist is not as obvious in the following selections as it was in the preceding monologues and parodies. Here, the author proceeds as if he is just telling a story, and his satiric intent is revealed more by the characters and events he creates than by his own tone of voice. You have already read a good example of satiric narrative, Alfred Bester's "Disappearing Act." You may recall how Bester remained in the background, allowing his details to speak for him.

Not all of the following selections are short stories; one is a poem, and two are often classified as essays. The form is unimportant. What concerns us here is the quality which marks these works as *satire*.

In this satiric essay, E. B. White has projected his imagination beyond the immediate and the factual into the realm of fiction. See if you can identify the point at which the truth ends and the fiction begins.

Irtnog

E. B. White

Along about 1920 it became apparent that more things were being written than people had time to read. That is to say, even if a man spent his entire time reading stories, articles, and news, as they appeared in books, magazines, and pamphlets, he fell behind. This was no fault of the reading public; on the contrary, readers made a real effort to keep pace with writers, and utilized every spare moment during their waking hours. They read while shaving in the morning and while waiting for trains and while riding on trains. There came to be a kind of tacit agreement among members of the reading public that when one person laid down the baton, someone else must pick it up; and so when a customer entered a barbershop, the barber would lay aside the Boston *Evening Globe* and the customer would pick up *Judge*;[1] or when a customer appeared in a shoeshining parlor, the bootblack would put away the *Racing Forum* and the customer would open his briefcase and pull out *The Sheik*. So there was always somebody reading something. Motormen of trolley cars read while they waited on the switch. Errand boys read while walking from the corner of Thirty-ninth and Madison to the corner of Twenty-fifth and Broadway. Subway riders read constantly, even when they were in a crushed, upright position in which nobody could read his own paper but everyone could look over the next man's shoulder. People passing newsstands would pause for a second to read headlines. Men in the back seats of limousines, northbound on Lafayette Street in the evening, switched on tiny dome lights and read the *Wall Street Journal*. Women in semi-detached houses joined circulating libraries and read Vachel Lindsay while the baby was taking his nap.

There was a tremendous volume of stuff that had to be read. Writing began to give off all sorts of by-products. Readers not only had

[1] *Judge:* a humorous magazine no longer published

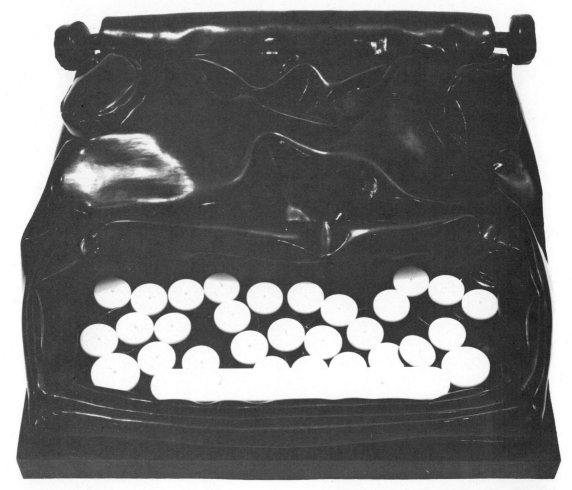

Claus Oldenburg

The Satiric Voice

58

to read the original works of a writer, but they also had to scan what the critics said, and they had to read advertisements reprinting the favorable criticisms, and they had to read the book chat giving some rather odd piece of information about the writer — such as that he could write only when he had a gingersnap in his mouth. It all took time. Writers gained steadily, and readers lost.

Then along came the *Reader's Digest*. That was a wonderful idea. It digested everything that was being written in leading magazines, and put new hope in the hearts of readers. Here, everybody thought, was the answer to the problem. Readers, badly discouraged by the rate they had been losing ground, took courage and set out once more to keep abreast of everything that was being written in the world. For a while they seemed to hold their own. But soon other digests and short cuts appeared, like *Time*, and *The Best Short Stories of 1927*, and the new Five-Foot Shelf,[2] and Wells's *Outline of History*, and *Newsweek*, and *Fiction Parade*. By 1939 there were one hundred and seventy-three digests, or short cuts, in America, and even if a man read nothing but digests of selected material, and read continuously, he couldn't keep up. It was obvious that something more concentrated than digests would have to come along to take up the slack.

It did. Someone conceived the idea of digesting the digests. He brought out a little publication called *Pith*, no bigger than your thumb. It was a digest of *Reader's Digest, Time, Concise Spicy Tales*, and the daily News Summary of the New York *Herald Tribune*. Everything was so extremely condensed that a reader could absorb everything that was being published in the world in about forty-five minutes. It was a tremendous financial success, and of course other publications sprang up, aping it: one called *Core*, another called *Nub*, and a third called *Nutshell*. *Nutshell* folded up, because, an expert said, the name was too long; but half a dozen others sprang up to take its place, and for another short period readers enjoyed a breathing spell and managed to stay abreast of writers. In fact, at one juncture, soon after the appearance of *Nub*, some person of unsound business tendencies felt that the digest rage had been carried too far and that there would be room in the magazine field for a counter-digest — a publication devoted to restoring literary bulk. He raised some money and issued a huge thing called *Amplifo*, undigesting the digests. In the second issue the name had been changed to *Regurgitans*. The third issue never

[2] *Five-Foot Shelf:* another name for the *Harvard Classics*, a collection of over four hundred literary masterpieces. This set occupies only five feet of shelf space.

reached the stands. *Pith* and *Core* continued to gain, and became so extraordinarily profitable that hundreds of other digests of digests came into being. Again readers felt themselves slipping. *Distillate* came along, a superdigest which condensed a Hemingway novel to the single word "Bang!" and reduced a long article about the problem of the unruly child to the words "Hit him."

You would think that with such drastic condensation going on, the situation would have resolved itself and that an adjustment would have been set up between writer and reader. Unfortunately, writers still forged ahead. Digests and superdigests, because of their rich returns, became as numerous as the things digested. It was not until 1960, when a Stevens Tech graduate named Abe Shapiro stepped in with an immense ingenious formula, that a permanent balance was established between writers and readers. Shapiro was a sort of Einstein. He had read prodigiously; and as he thought back over all the things that he had ever read, he became convinced that it would be possible to express them in mathematical quintessence. He was positive that he could take everything that was written and published each day, and reduce it to a six-letter word. He worked out a secret formula and began posting daily bulletins, telling his result. Everything that had been written during the first day of his formula came down to the word "Irtnog." The second day, everything reduced to "Efsitz." People accepted these mathematical distillations; and strangely enough, or perhaps not strangely at all, people were thoroughly satisfied—which would lead one to believe that what readers really craved was not so much the contents of books, magazines, and papers as the assurance that they were not missing anything. Shapiro found that his bulletin board was inadequate, so he made a deal with a printer and issued a handbill at five o'clock every afternoon, giving the Word of the Day. It caught hold instantly.

The effect on the populace was salutary. Readers, once they felt confident that they had one-hundred-per-cent coverage, were able to discard the unnatural habit of focusing their eyes on words every instant. Freed of the exhausting consequences of their hopeless race against writers, they found their health returning, along with a certain tranquillity and a more poised way of living. There was a marked decrease in stomach ulcers, which, doctors said, had been the result of allowing the eye to jump nervously from one newspaper headline to another after a heavy meal. With the dwindling of reading, writing fell off. Forests, which had been plundered for newsprint, grew tall again; droughts were unheard of; and people dwelt in slow comfort, in a green world.

QUESTIONS FOR DISCUSSION

1. How does White give you a sense of the overwhelming number of things being written and published?
2. What does White think of *Reader's Digest, Time, The Best Short Stories of 1927,* "the new Five-Foot Shelf," Wells's *Outline of History, Newsweek,* and *Fiction Parade?*
3. At what point in his narrative does White begin to indulge in total fabrication?
4. You have seen how useful exaggeration can be to the satirist. When he embellishes and distorts the truth so that it seems fantastic, he leads the reader to see that the truth actually *is* fantastic, ridiculous, perhaps even ominous. What is the "truth" behind White's essay?
5. What are the names of the digests that White says appeared after 1939? What do these names mean?
6. Why does White say that "what readers really craved was not so much the contents of the books, magazines, and papers as the assurance that they were not missing anything"?
7. Is "Irtnog" a workable substitute for a day's worth of writing? What is White saying about digests in general?
8. The subject of "Irtnog" is very much like that of Russell Baker's "The Disposable Man." What similarities and differences do you see between Baker's manner of presentation and White's?

White used a kind of *anticlimax* when he moved from reality to fiction in his essay. *Anticlimax* occurs when an author leads us to expect one thing and then gives us something quite different. As you read the remaining selections, watch for other examples of anticlimax used as a satiric device.

Earth

John Hall Wheelock

"A planet doesn't explode of itself," said drily
The Martian astronomer, gazing off into the air—
"That they were able to do it is proof that highly
Intelligent beings must have been living there."

1. Why does Wheelock use a *persona* (a fictitious character who expresses the author's views) in this poem? What do we know about the speaker and his point of view?
2. Does anticlimax operate in this poem? If so, explain how it works.
3. Does the Martian astronomer's "proof" prove what he says it does?
4. What common literary device provides the basis of the satiric effect of this poem?

You may have seen Art Buchwald's syndicated column on the editorial page of your newspaper. As you read "Mars is *Ours!*" remember that Buchwald writes for a large, popular audience. Notice how he uses satire to combine the qualities of the editorial and the narrative.

Mars Is *Ours!*

Art Buchwald

When it was discovered by American and Russian space probes that there was indeed life on Mars, an immediate foreign ministers' conference in Geneva was called to decide what to do about it.

The United States, through its Secretary of State, announced that America had no territorial designs on the planet and the U.S. position was that the Martians should be free to choose their own government, providing of course that it was not Communist-dominated or leftist-inspired.

The Soviet minister said that if the Martians wanted to overthrow the reactionary rulers who were probably exploiting the Martian masses, his country would have no choice but to come to their aid. He said that if the Martians requested it, the Soviet Union would supply them with planes, rockets, and up-to-date radar.

The United States said that if the Soviet Union interfered, it would have no choice but to send Marines to Mars to protect the lives of free Martians as well as American tourists who would soon be visiting there.

The real problem was that nobody knew what kind of government the Martians had.

All the photographs showed that there was life on Mars, but unfortunately there were no flags in the pictures to indicate where the Martians stood.

Both the Soviet Union and the United States were at a stalemate until someone came up with a brilliant solution.

Mars would be divided in half. The northern part would be known as North Viet-Mars and the south would be known as South Viet-Mars.

The Soviets would be in charge of the North, the U.S. in charge of the South, and free elections would be promised within two years of partition.

The United States immediately set up a Mars aid program to give the Martians economic and financial assistance when the time came. It also trained military-assistance teams which would land with the aid people and train the Martians in defense against the North.

The Soviets divided North Viet-Mars into communes and trained political commissars and technicians to go into the country and communize it.

Irtnog

In the meantime, Communist China, which had not been asked to the conference, started making its own plans for Mars. It announced an Afro-Asian-Mars Conference to take place in Peking, where both the Western "bandits" and the Soviet "deviationists" would be attacked. China said, as soon as it had enough spaceships, it would send one million Chinese volunteers to Mars to save the planet from American and Soviet imperialism.

Although the French had nothing to do with the space explorations, they insisted Mars should become part of a Third Force under the direction of General de Gaulle.

Unbeknownst to the great powers on Earth, the Martians were holding a summit meeting of their own on the Mars Bar Canal.

"Then it is agreed upon," the Grand Clyde of Mare Cimmerium said. "We shall set up an East Earth and a West Earth. We shall have the East, and Trivium Charontis will have the West."

The Trivium Charontis Super Zilch said, "We shall hold elections within two years and let the Earth people decide for themselves what form of government they want."

"I cannot state strongly enough," said the Grand Clyde of Mare Cimmerium, "that if Trivium Charontis does anything to violate the treaty we will be forced to use all the weapons at our disposal."

"And I can assure you, Grand Clyde, Trivium Charontis will not stand by and see West Earthlings swallowed up by Mare Cimmerium. If need be, we shall use the clong."

The Grand Clyde said, "We shall see which system prevails."

QUESTIONS FOR DISCUSSION

1. Is the technical point of view in "Mars is *Ours!*" the same as in "Earth"? Explain any differences that you see.
2. Compare the Martians and the Earthlings. What plans do they make for each other? What do you think the "clong" is?
3. Explain the irony in this narrative.
4. Is anticlimax involved here? If so, explain how it works.
5. Do you think Buchwald meant this narrative as a science-fiction representation of what might really happen if we discover life on Mars, or is he doing something else here? What is Buchwald saying about people and nations?

"I Can't Breathe" illustrated how the realities of love and marriage may be distorted by an egotist with "romantic" illusions. In the following story, people behave according to their own concepts of reality, only to find that things are not nearly as simple as they had thought.

Who's Passing for Who?

Langston Hughes

One of the great difficulties about being a member of a minority race is that so many kindhearted, well-meaning bores gather around to help. Usually, to tell the truth, they have nothing to help with, except their company—which is often appallingly dull.

Some members of the Negro race seem very well able to put up with it, though, in these uplifting years. Such was Caleb Johnson, colored social worker, who was always dragging around with him some nondescript white person or two, inviting them to dinner, showing them Harlem, ending up at the Savoy—much to the displeasure of whatever friends of his might be out that evening for fun, not sociology.

Friends are friends and, unfortunately, overearnest uplifters are uplifters—no matter what color they may be. If it were the white race that was ground down instead of Negroes, Caleb Johnson would be one of the first to offer Nordics the sympathy of his utterly inane society, under the impression that somehow he would be doing them a great deal of good.

You see, Caleb, and his white friends, too, were all bores. Or so we, who lived in Harlem's literary bohemia during the "Negro Renaissance" thought. We literary ones considered ourselves too broadminded to be bothered with questions of color. We liked people of any race who smoked incessantly, drank liberally, wore complexion and morality as loose garments, and made fun of anyone who didn't do likewise. We snubbed and high-hatted any Negro or white luckless enough not to understand Gertrude Stein, *Ulysses*, Man Ray, the theremin,[1] Jean Toomer, or George Antheil. By the end of the 1920's Caleb was just catching up to Dos Passos. He thought H. G. Wells good.

[1] *theremin:* an electronic musical instrument.

We met Caleb one night at Small's. He had three assorted white folks in tow. We would have passed him by with but a nod had he not hailed us enthusiastically, risen, and introduced us with great acclaim to his friends who turned out to be schoolteachers from Iowa, a woman and two men. They appeared amazed and delighted to meet all at once two Negro writers and a black painter in the flesh. They invited us to have a drink with them. Money being scarce with us, we deigned to sit down at their table.

The white lady said, "I've never met a Negro writer before."

The two men added, "Neither have we."

"Why, we know any number of *white* writers," we three dark bohemians declared with bored nonchalance.

"But Negro writers are much more rare," said the lady.

"There are plenty in Harlem," we said.

"But not in Iowa," said one of the men, shaking his mop of red hair.

"There are no good *white* writers in Iowa either, are there?" we asked superciliously.

"Oh, yes, Ruth Suckow came from there."

Whereupon we proceeded to light in upon Ruth Suckow as old hat and to annihilate her in favor of Kay Boyle. The way we flung names around seemed to impress both Caleb and his white guests. This, of course, delighted us, though we were too young and too proud to admit it.

The drinks came and everything was going well, all of us drinking, and we three showing off in a high-brow manner, when suddenly at the table just behind us a man got up and knocked down a woman. He was a brownskin man. The woman was blonde. As she rose he knocked her down again. Then the red-haired man from Iowa got up and knocked the colored man down.

He said, "Keep your hands off that white woman."

The man got up and said, "She's not a white woman. She's my wife."

One of the waiters added, "She's not white, sir, she's colored."

Whereupon the man from Iowa looked puzzled, dropped his fists, and said, "I'm sorry."

The colored man said, "What are you doing up here in Harlem anyway, interfering with my family affairs?"

The white man said, "I thought she was a white woman."

The woman who had been on the floor rose and said, "Well, I'm not a white woman, I'm colored, and you leave my husband alone."

Then they both lit in on the gentleman from Iowa. It took all of us and several waiters, too, to separate them. When it was over the manager requested us to kindly pay our bill and get out. He said we were disturbing the peace. So we all left. We went to a fish restaurant down the street. Caleb was terribly apologetic to his white friends. We artists were both mad and amused.

"Why did you say you were sorry," said the colored painter to the visitor from Iowa, "after you'd hit that man — and then found out it wasn't a white woman you were defending, but merely a light colored woman who looked white?"

"Well," answered the red-haired Iowan, "I didn't mean to be butting in if they were all the same race."

"Don't you think a woman needs defending from a brute, no matter what race she may be?" asked the painter.

"Yes, but I think it's up to you to defend your own women."

"Oh, so you'd divide up a brawl according to races, no matter who was right?"

"Well, I wouldn't say that."

"You mean you wouldn't defend a colored woman whose husband was knocking her down?" asked the poet.

Before the visitor had time to answer, the painter said, "No! You just got mad because you thought a black man was hitting a *white* woman."

"But she *looked* like a white woman," countered the man.

"Maybe she was just passing for colored," I said.

"Like some Negroes pass for white," Caleb interposed.

"Anyhow, I don't like it," said the colored painter, "the way you stopped defending her when you found out she wasn't white."

"No, we don't like it," we all agreed except Caleb.

Caleb said in extenuation, "But Mr. Stubblefield is new to Harlem."

The red-haired white man said, "Yes, it's my first time here."

"Maybe Mr. Stubblefield ought to stay out of Harlem," we observed.

"I agree," Mr. Stubblefield said. "Good night."

He got up then and there and left the café. He stalked as he walked. His red head disappeared into the night.

"Oh, that's too bad," said the white couple who remained. "Stubby's temper just got the best of him. But explain to us, are many colored folks really as fair as that woman?"

"Sure, lots of them have more white blood than colored, and pass for white."

"Do they?" said the lady and gentleman from Iowa.

"You never read Nella Larsen?" we asked.

"She writes novels," Caleb explained. "She's part white herself."

"Read her," we advised. "Also read the *Autobiography of an Ex-Colored Man.*" Not that we had read it ourselves—because we paid but little attention to the older colored writers—but we knew it was about passing for white.

We all ordered fish and settled down comfortably to shocking our white friends with tales about how many Negroes there were passing for white all over America. We were determined to *épater le bourgeois* real good via this white couple we had cornered, when the woman leaned over the table in the midst of our dissertations and said, "Listen, gentlemen, you needn't spread the word, but me and my husband aren't white either. We've just been *passing* for white for the last fifteen years."

"What?"

"We're colored, too, just like you," said the husband. "But it's better passing for white because we make more money."

Well, that took the wind out of us. It took the wind out of Caleb, too. He thought all the time he was showing some fine white folks Harlem —and they were as colored as he was!

Then everybody laughed. And laughed! We almost had hysterics.

All at once we dropped our professionally self-conscious "Negro" manners, became natural, ate fish, and talked and kidded freely like colored folks do when there are no white folks around. We really had fun then, joking about that red-haired guy who mistook a fair colored woman for white. After the fish we went to two or three more night spots and drank until five o'clock in the morning.

Finally we put the light-colored people in a taxi heading downtown. They turned to shout a last good-by. The cab was just about to move off, when the woman called to the driver to stop.

She leaned out the window and said with a grin, "Listen, boys! I hate to confuse you again. But, to tell the truth, my husband and I aren't really colored at all. We're white. We just thought we'd kid you by passing for colored a little while—just as you said Negroes sometimes pass for white."

She laughed as they sped off toward Central Park, waving, "Good-by!"

We didn't say a thing. We just stood there on the corner in Harlem dumbfounded—not knowing now *which* way we'd been fooled. Were they really white — passing for colored? Or colored — passing for white?"

Whatever race they were, they had had too much fun at our expense—even if they did pay for the drinks.

QUESTIONS FOR DISCUSSION

1. How does the narrator feel about Caleb Johnson?
2. Identify all of the characters in this story. Which ones "pass" for something else? Which ones alter their behavior when they are informed of someone's "real" identity? When are the characters most comfortable?
3. Where is the climax of this story?
4. Does anticlimax operate in the story? Explain.
5. Briefly state the meaning of this story as you think the author intends it.
6. Considering all of the material you have read so far, including Swift's verse on satire, formulate your own definition of satire. How well does this story fit your definition?

The Writer's Style

This story contains references to a number of literary and artistic figures. It is not important for the reader to know all about the people or the individual works as it is for him to understand why the allusions are included. Why is a knowledge of these matters important to the speaker and his friends? How do they use this knowledge as a social index?

SUGGESTIONS FOR COMPOSITION

1. In essay form, discuss any of the satiric narratives you have read in this section in terms of the specific satiric devices employed by the author. Consider irony, sarcasm, understatement, hyperbole, burlesque humor, a mock-heroic approach, anti-climax.
2. Write a satiric narrative, in prose or verse, in which you "push" an aspect of contemporary American culture into the realm of absurdity in order to reveal the absurdity of the actual situation.

Anthology

In the following selections, you will find some more examples of how authors use humor or an indirect method of presentation to make criticisms of the way men live and the values they hold. As in the essays, poems, and narratives you just read, some of these criticisms will be relatively light or humorous; others will be bitter or even frightening.

Remember, as you read and discuss what follows, that the writer of satire always requires his readers to think hard about the things he is criticizing. If they do not respond to his interpretations, he cannot achieve his purpose of inspiring a desire for reform.

The writers in the following anthology cover a wide variety of subjects: political manipulation in our nation's capital; the dangers of too much technology or too much dependence on machines; the common human vices of envy, greed, and self-deception. As you read each selection, ask yourself the following questions: What, actually, is the author criticizing about society? What basic attitude does he have toward his subject? What satiric devices (exaggeration, irony, false identity) does he use to make us aware of his attitude? For instance, what effect does Hoppe gain by implying from the beginning of his essay that Washington, D.C., is a separate country from the rest of the U.S., and that it is "surrounded on all four sides by reality"? What is the meaning of the poem recited in Bradbury's story? How does Bierce use his various word definitions to comment critically on human values and actions?

The writer of satire asks us to make up our own minds about the kind of world we live in. If we answer his challenge by playing off our own attitudes against his, we come to know better not only our society, but ourselves. Hopefully, the following selections will stimulate you in that direction.

Interesting Native Customs
in Washington and
Other Savage Lands

Arthur Hoppe

When visiting a strange country like Washington, it's incumbent on us responsible ace newsmen to file what we call "a backgrounder." You know, a lengthy review of annual rainfall and grazing conditions with a few paragraphs about quaint native courting customs thrown in to sex things up a little.

Well, Washington is several miles square and about as tall, say, as the Washington Monument, give or take a little. It is surrounded on all four sides by reality. The winters aren't too hot. Neither is the rest of the climate. The natives, in general, are sullen.

While the outside world refers to it as "Washington," the natives call it "the District," short for "District of Columbia." And the natives, of course, do not think of themselves as "natives." They think of themselves as "experts." The population, at the moment, consists of 998,762 experts and two tourists from Camden, Ohio, who, on being interviewed, said they hadn't the foggiest notion of what was wrong with U.S. foreign policy.

The main industries are eating, drinking, and talking. The major import and export—indeed, the staple of the economy—is money. As with many other countries these days, Washington imports more from us than it exports. This creates what we economists call "an unfavorable trade balance." Which, in this case, it certainly is.

The local unit of currency is "the Million Dollar." Usually written "$1 million." Many of these, however, are required to purchase anything. So they are generally referred to in the plural, such as "thus and so many Million Dollars." In recent years, a new denomination, "the Billion Dollar" (written "$1 billion") has come into wide use. And lately one even hears "the Trillion Dollar" mentioned on occasion. But only in referring to the national debt.

It is exceedingly difficult to calculate a rate of exchange between Washington money and our money because the essential characteristic of Washington money is that it's not real. No native, to my knowledge, has ever seen "a Million Dollar," much less "a Billion Dollar," although they remain the chief topic of conversation.

Lesser denominations, such as "the Thousand Dollar" or "the Hundred Dollar" have, like the old French centime, virtually disappeared from circulation. And the only place the natives use real money, such as the dollar, is after office hours. Indeed, any mention of real money tends for some unexplained reason to make the natives restless. Take, for example, the case of the underground garage.

The Solons, a local tribe living on Capitol Hill, recently decided to build an underground garage so their cars wouldn't get sunburned. This would cost only four "Million Dollars," and everybody was quite content. But then someone, presumably an anthropologist from the real world, announced, after much calculation, that this figure came to somewhere around $25,000 per car. Which sounded like real money. And it was suggested that the Solons might economize by merely buying cheap cars and throwing them away each day on arriving at their meeting place. This talk about real money made the Solons terribly nervous. Not nervous enough, of course, to cancel their plans for the four "Million Dollar" garage. But terribly nervous.

Despite the obvious need for a drastic currency reform, however, the local economy is booming. Everywhere the visitor looks, new buildings are going up. And when you realize that the natives neither manufacture nor produce anything of salable value, this expansion is all the more fantastic.

The new buildings are, of course, all being constructed in the Four-square Monolithic Style of modern native architecture. The natives, it is believed, pour a solid cube of concrete, hollow out the inside, and stick a flagpole on top. The result, it is generally agreed, is much more permanent than the thatched huts of the Wambeesi. If not as pleasing to the eye.

But it is certainly clear to even the most casual observer that all this activity indicates the natives, due to our help, have at last reached "the economic takeoff point." And while my heart goes out to them in their struggle to better themselves, I feel it is now our grim duty to cut back drastically on our financial-aid program so that they may learn to stand on their own two feet. I feel strongly that we should take this step before April 15 at the latest.

Let us now turn to the social structure of the country. As in many of the new African nations, the natives of Washington belong not to one, but to numerous separate and distinct tribes, each spiritedly warlike and fiercely jealous of its prerogatives. The best known of the local tribes are, of course, the Solons, occupying the strategic heights of Capitol Hill, and the Presidents, who live on the flats perhaps a mile away. . . . Lesser known are the numerous other interesting tribes of the flats, such as "State," "Commerce," "Interior," "NRA" (now extinct), and so forth. While nominally joined by treaty with the Presidents, these lesser tribes devote most of their energies to battling each other. . . .

The young warriors of each tribe are prepared for leadership in these devious wars by a rite known as Shafting—a test similar to the trial-by-fire dance for young Ugulaps in North Borneo. Unlike the fire dance, which is a one-time fling for the young Ugulap, Shafting remains the prime occupation of the Washingtonian from his entry into the tribe until his death or retirement.

The goal in the rites of Shafting is telephone buttons. A telephone without buttons is a symbol of shame, and the native who has one invariably keeps it turned away from his visitors. A phone with two buttons is the symbol of having arrived at manhood, and so forth on up. Status is carefully equated. A six-button native, for instance, would never telephone a four-button native. Except through his secretary. The current scepter of chiefhood in all tribes is a conference phone, a light green model with chromium hooks and no fewer than eighteen plastic buttons, two of them red. With this goes a corner office, a conference table, two flags in standards, and four in-and-out baskets.

Most of the inordinately complex rituals of Shafting are fathomable only by anthropologists. Three of the simpler forms will be discussed here: Leaking, Copy-to-ing and Jack Hornering.

Leaking is practiced only at the highest levels in each tribe. Usually by subchieftans. When a mistake is made, Subchief X announces quickly that no mistake was made. Then he Leaks the inside information to the Columnists (a tribe of local historians of tremendous unimportance) that in reality it was a horrendous mistake. And that Subchief Y made it. When three or more Columnists print the leak, it becomes known as a *fact*. And Subchief Y is stripped of one secretary, his leather couch, and four buttons from his telephone. . . .

Copy-to-ing is practiced on the lower levels. Should Al Z, a young native working under Chief Y, make a minor slip, he will immediately receive fourteen interoffice memos from his fellow tribesmen. Such as: "Al, I was very sorry to see us get in that awful bind. But I did warn you at Staff beforehand. How about talking it over? Perhaps something can still be saved from the wreckage."

At the bottom of each memo is typed: COPY TO CHIEF Y. While no chief could possibly read all the scores of copies of memos he receives each day, the psychological damage on Al Z of those words, COPY TO CHIEF Y, can well be imagined.

I stumbled on Jack Hornering by making friends with a young native barely of the Executive Dining Room level. I found him busily initialing each page of an eight-page report to his chief.

"It cuts the chance of being Jack Hornered," he said.

Jack Hornered? "Sure," he said. "This report's loaded with good ideas. And it's got to pass through a lot of hands on its way to the top. Each hand's got a thumb. Remember? 'So he stuck in his thumb and pulled out a plum and said, "What a good boy am I." ' Sometimes an eight-page report gets to the top saying nothing but: 'Dear Chief: Yrs Truly.' I figure if I initial every page it will be a psychological burglar lock. To tell you the truth, though," he added gloomily, "it never works."

In my forthcoming book, *Interesting Native Customs in Washington and Other Savage Lands*, I've decided to prepare the gentler readers for the bloody accounts of Washington tribal shafting by building up to them gradually. For example, the early chapters will deal with less gruesome customs of more civilized tribes. Like: "Disembowelment Techniques Among the Mau Mau."

With all this intertribal and intratribal warfare, the natives, understandably enough, have little interest in the outside world, except as its events affect their internecine quarrels. Indeed, many modern anthropologists feel that if the natives could ever be knit into one homogeneous unit, their skill and deviousness in the arts of warfare would inevitably mean that Washington would soon come to rule the world.

As of now, however, this danger appears extremely remote.

A Caution to Everybody

Ogden Nash

Consider the auk;
Becoming extinct because he forgot how to fly, and could only
walk.
Consider man, who may well become extinct
Because he forgot how to walk and learned how to fly before he
thinked.

There Will Come Soft Rains

Ray Bradbury

In the living room the voice-clock sang, *Tick-tock, seven o'clock, time to get up, time to get up, seven o'clock!* as if it were afraid that nobody would. The morning house lay empty. The clock ticked on, repeating and repeating its sounds into the emptiness. *Seven-nine, breakfast time, seven-nine!*

In the kitchen the breakfast stove gave a hissing sigh and ejected from its warm interior eight pieces of perfectly browned toast, eight eggs sunnyside up, sixteen slices of bacon, two coffees, and two cool glasses of milk.

"Today is August 4, 2026," said a second voice from the kitchen ceiling, "in the city of Allendale, California." It repeated the date three times for memory's sake. "Today is Mr. Featherstone's birthday. Today is the anniversary of Tilita's marriage. Insurance is payable, as are the water, gas, and light bills."

Somewhere in the walls, relays clicked, memory tapes glided under electric eyes.

Eight-one, tick-tock, eight-one o'clock, off to school, off to work, run, run, eight-one! But no doors slammed, no carpets took the soft tread of rubber heels. It was raining outside. The weather box on the front door sang quietly: "Rain, rain, go away; rubbers, raincoats for today ..." And the rain tapped on the empty house, echoing.

Outside, the garage chimed and lifted its door to reveal the waiting car. After a long wait the door swung down again.

At eight-thirty the eggs were shriveled and the toast was like stone. An aluminum wedge scraped them into the sink, where hot water whirled them down a metal throat which digested and flushed them away to the distant sea. The dirty dishes were dropped into a hot washer and emerged twinkling dry.

Nine-fifteen, sang the clock, *time to clean.*

Out of warrens in the wall, tiny robot mice darted. The rooms were acrawl with the small cleaning animals, all rubber and metal. They thudded against chairs, whirling their mustached runners, kneading the rug nap, sucking gently at hidden dust.

Then, like mysterious invaders, they popped into their burrows. Their pink electric eyes faded. The house was clean.

Ten o'clock. The sun came out from behind the rain. The house stood alone in a city of rubble and ashes. This was the one house left standing. At night the ruined city gave off a radioactive glow which could be seen for miles.

Ten-fifteen. The garden sprinklers whirled up in golden founts, filling the soft morning air with scatterings of brightness. The water pelted windowpanes, running down the charred west side where the house had been burned evenly free of its white paint. The entire west face of the house was black, save for five places. Here the silhouette in paint of a man mowing a lawn. Here, as in a photograph, a woman bent to pick flowers. Still farther over, their images burned on wood in one titanic instant, a small boy, hands flung into the air; higher up, the image of a thrown ball, and opposite him a girl, hands raised to catch a ball which never came down.

The five spots of paint—the man, the woman, the children, the ball—remained. The rest was a thin charcoaled layer.

There Will Come Soft Rains

The gentle sprinkler rain filled the garden with falling light.

Until this day, how well the house had kept its peace. How carefully it had inquired, "Who goes there? What's the password?" and, getting no answer from lonely foxes and whining cats, it had shut up its windows and drawn shades in an old-maidenly preoccupation with self-protection which bordered on a mechanical paranoia.

It quivered at each sound, the house did. If a sparrow brushed a window, the shade snapped up. The bird, startled, flew off! No, not even a bird must touch the house!

The house was an altar with ten thousand attendants, big, small, servicing, attending, in choirs. But the gods had gone away, and the ritual of the religion continued senselessly, uselessly.

Twelve noon.

A dog whined, shivering, on the front porch.

The front door recognized the dog voice and opened. The dog, once huge and fleshy, but now gone to bone and covered with sores, moved in and through the house, tracking mud. Behind it whirred angry mice, angry at having to pick up mud, angry at inconvenience.

For not a leaf fragment blew under the door but what the wall panels flipped open and the copper scrap-rats flashed swiftly out. The offending dust, hair, or paper, seized in miniature steel jaws, was raced back to the burrows. There, down tubes which fed into the cellar, it was dropped into the sighing vent of an incinerator which sat like evil Baal in a dark corner.

The dog ran upstairs, hysterically yelping to each door, at last realizing, as the house realized, that only silence was here.

It sniffed the air and scratched the kitchen door. Behind the door, the stove was making pancakes which filled the house with a rich baked odor and the scent of maple syrup.

The dog frothed at the mouth, lying at the door, sniffing, its eyes turned to fire. It ran wildly in circles, biting at its tail, spun in a frenzy, and died. It lay in the parlor for an hour.

Two o'clock, sang a voice.

Delicately sensing decay at last, the regiments of mice hummed out as softly as blown gray leaves in an electrical wind.

Two-fifteen.

The dog was gone.

In the cellar, the incinerator glowed suddenly and a whirl of sparks leaped up the chimney.

Two thirty-five.

Bridge tables sprouted from patio walls. Playing cards fluttered onto pads in a shower of pips. Martinis manifested on an oaken bench with egg-salad sandwiches. Music played.

But the tables were silent and the cards untouched.

At four o'clock the tables folded like great butterflies back through the paneled walls.

Four-thirty.

The nursery walls glowed.

Animals took shape: yellow giraffes, blue lions, pink antelopes, lilac panthers cavorting in crystal substance. The walls were glass. They looked out upon color and fantasy. Hidden films clocked through well-oiled sprockets, and the walls lived. The nursery floor was woven to resemble a crisp cereal meadow. Over this ran aluminum roaches and iron crickets, and in the hot still air butterflies of delicate red tissue wavered among the sharp aroma of animal spoors! There was the sound like a great matted yellow hive of bees within a dark bellows, the lazy bumble of a purring lion. And there was the patter of okapi feet and the murmur of a fresh jungle rain, like other hoofs, falling upon the summer-starched grass. Now the walls dissolved into distances of parched weed, mile on mile, and warm endless sky. The animals drew away into thorn brakes and water holes.

It was the children's hour.

Five o'clock. The bath filled with clear hot water.

Six, seven, eight o'clock. The dinner dishes manipulated like magic tricks, and in the study a *click*. In the metal stand opposite the hearth where a fire now blazed up warmly, a cigar popped out, half an inch of soft gray ash on it, smoking, waiting.

Nine o'clock. The beds warmed their hidden circuits, for nights were cool here.

Nine-five. A voice spoke from the study ceiling:

"Mrs. McClellan, which poem would you like this evening?"

The house was silent.

The voice said at last, "Since you express no preference, I shall select a poem at random." Quiet music rose to back the voice. "Sara Teasdale. As I recall, your favorite. . . .

"There will come soft rains and the smell of the ground,
And swallows circling with their shimmering sound;

And frogs in the pools singing at night,
And wild plum trees in tremulous white;

Robins will wear their feathery fire,
Whistling their whims on a low fence-wire;

And not one will know of the war, not one
Will care at last when it is done.

Not one would mind, neither bird nor tree,
If mankind perished utterly;

And Spring herself, when she woke at dawn
Would scarcely know that we were gone."

The fire burned on the stone hearth and the cigar fell away into a mound of quiet ash on its tray. The empty chairs faced each other between the silent walls, and the music played.

At ten o'clock the house began to die.

The wind blew. A falling tree bough crashed through the kitchen window. Cleaning solvent, bottled, shattered over the stove. The room was ablaze in an instant!

"Fire!" screamed a voice. The house lights flashed, water pumps shot water from the ceilings. But the solvent spread on the linoleum, licking, eating, under the kitchen door, while the voices took it up in chorus: "Fire, fire, fire!"

The house tried to save itself. Doors sprang tightly shut, but the windows were broken by the heat and the wind blew and sucked upon the fire.

The house gave ground as the fire in ten billion angry sparks moved with flaming ease from room to room and then up the stairs. While scurrying water rats squeaked from the walls, pistoled their water, and ran for more. And the wall sprays let down showers of mechanical rain.

But too late. Somewhere, sighing, a pump shrugged to a stop. The quenching rain ceased. The reserve water supply which had filled baths and washed dishes for many quiet days was gone.

The fire crackled up the stairs. It fed upon Picassos and Matisses in the upper halls, like delicacies, baking off the oily flesh, tenderly crisping the canvases into black shavings.

Now the fire lay in beds, stood in windows, changed the colors of drapes!

And then, reinforcements.

From attic trapdoors, blind robot faces peered down with faucet mouths gushing green chemical.

The fire backed off, as even an elephant must at the sight of a dead snake. Now there were twenty snakes whipping over the floor, killing the fire with a clear cold venom of green froth.

But the fire was clever. It had sent flame outside the house, up through the attic to the pumps there. An explosion! The attic brain which directed the pumps was shattered into bronze shrapnel on the beams.

The fire rushed back into every closet and felt of the clothes hung there.

The house shuddered, oak bone on bone, its bared skeleton cringing from the heat, its wire, its nerves revealed as if a surgeon had torn the skin off to let the red veins and capillaries quiver in the scalded air. Help, help! Fire! Run, run! Heat snapped mirrors like the first brittle winter ice. And the voices wailed, Fire, fire, run, run, like a tragic nursery rhyme, a dozen voices, high, low, like children dying in a forest, alone, alone. And the voices fading as the wires popped their sheathings like hot chestnuts. One, two, three, four, five voices died.

In the nursery the jungle burned. Blue lions roared, purple giraffes bounded off. The panthers ran in circles, changing color, and ten million animals, running before the fire, vanished off toward a distant steaming river. . . .

Ten more voices died. In the last instant under the fire avalanche, other choruses, oblivious, could be heard announcing the time, playing music, cutting the lawn by remote-control mower, or setting an umbrella frantically out and in the slamming and opening front door, a thousand things happening, like a clock shop when each clock strikes the hour insanely before or after the other, a scene of maniac confusion, yet unity; singing, screaming, a few last cleaning mice darting bravely out to carry the horrid ashes away! And one voice, with sublime disregard for the situation, read poetry aloud in the fiery study, until all the film spools burned, until all the wires withered and the circuits cracked.

There Will Come Soft Rains

The fire burst the house and let it slam flat down, puffing out skirts of spark and smoke.

In the kitchen, an instant before the rain of fire and timber, the stove could be seen making breakfasts at a psychopathic rate, ten dozen eggs, six loaves of toast, twenty dozen bacon strips, which, eaten by fire, started the stove working again, hysterically hissing!

The crash. The attic smashing into kitchen and parlor. The parlor into cellar, cellar into subcellar. Deep freeze, armchair, film tapes, circuits, beds, and all like skeletons thrown in a cluttered mound deep under.

Smoke and silence. A great quantity of smoke.

Dawn showed faintly in the east. Among the ruins, one wall stood alone. Within the wall, a last voice said, over and over again and again, even as the sun rose to shine upon the heaped rubble and steam:

"Today is August 5, 2026, today is August 5, 2026, today is . . ."

Nightmare Number Three

Stephen Vincent Benét

We had expected everything but revolt
And I kind of wonder myself when they started thinking—
But there's no dice in that now.
                                    I've heard fellows say
They must have planned it for years and maybe they did.   5
Looking back, you can find little incidents here and there,
Like the concrete-mixer in Jersey eating the wop
Or the roto press that printed "Fiddle-dee-dee!"
In a three-color process all over Senator Sloop,
Just as he was making a speech. The thing about that   10
Was, how could it walk upstairs? But it *was* upstairs,
Clicking and mumbling in the Senate Chamber.
They had to knock out the wall to take it away
And the wrecking-crew said it grinned.
                                    It was only the best   15
Machines, of course, the superhuman machines,
The ones we'd built to be better than flesh and bone,
But the cars were in it, of course. . . .
                                    and they hunted us
Like rabbits through the cramped streets on that Bloody Monday,
The Madison Avenue buses leading the charge.   20
The buses were pretty bad—but I'll not forget
The smash of glass when the Duesenberg left the show-room
And pinned three brokers to the Racquet Club steps,
Or the long howl of the horns when they saw the men run,
When they saw them looking for holes in the solid ground . . .   25

I guess they were tired of being ridden in,
And stopped and started by pygmies for silly ends,
Of wrapping cheap cigarettes and bad chocolate bars,
Collecting nickels and waving platinum hair,
And letting six million people live in a town.   30
I guess it was that. I guess they got tired of us
And the whole smell of human hands.
                                    But it was a shock
To climb sixteen flights of stairs to Art Zuckow's office

(Nobody took the elevators twice) 35
And find him strangled to death in a nest of telephones,
The octopus-tendrils waving over his head,
And a sort of quiet humming filling the air ...
Do they eat? ... There was red ... But I did not stop to look.
And it's lonely, here on the roof. 40
                                        For a while I thought
That window-cleaner would make it, and keep me company.
But they got him with his own hoist at the sixteenth floor
And dragged him in with a squeal.
You see, they cooperate. Well, we taught them that, 45
And it's fair enough, I suppose. You see, we built them.
We taught them to think for themselves.
It was bound to come. You can see it was bound to come.
And it won't be so bad, in the country. I hate to think
Of the reapers, running wild in the Kansas fields, 50
And the transport planes like hawks on a chickenyard,
But the horses might help. We might make a deal with the horses.
At least you've more chance, out there.

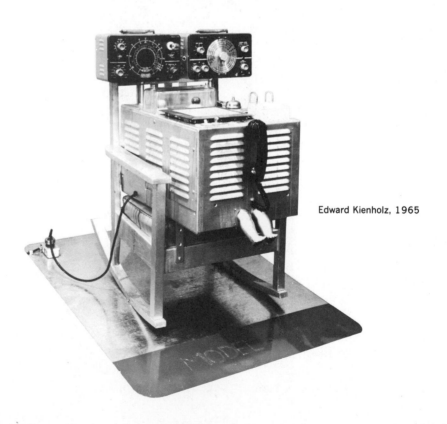

Edward Kienholz, 1965

And they need us too.

They're bound to realize that when they once calm down.   55
They'll need oil and spare parts and adjustments and tuning up.
Slaves? Well, in a way, you know, we were slaves before.
There won't be so much real difference—honest there won't.
(I wish I hadn't looked into that beauty-parlor
And seen what was happening there.   60
But those are female machines and a bit high-strung.)
Oh, we'll settle down. We'll arrange it. We'll compromise.
It wouldn't make sense to wipe out the whole human race.
Why, I bet if I went to my old Plymouth now
(Of course, you'd have to do it the tactful way)   65
And said, "Look here! Who got you the swell French horn?"
He wouldn't turn me over to those police cars.
At least I don't *think* he would.
Oh, it's going to be jake.

There won't be so much real difference—honest, there won't—   70
And I'd go down in a minute and take my chance—
I'm a good American and I always liked them—
Except for one small detail that bothers me
And that's the food proposition. Because you see,
The concrete-mixer may have made a mistake,   75
And it looks like just high spirits.
But, if it's got so they like the flavor ... well ...

FROM The Devil's Dictionary

Ambrose Bierce

absurdity, *n.* A statement or belief manifestly inconsistent with one's own opinion.

academe, *n.* An ancient school where morality and philosophy were taught.

academy, *n.* (from academe). A modern school where football is taught.

accident, *n.* An inevitable occurrence due to the action of immutable natural laws.

acquaintance, *n.*   A person whom we know well enough to borrow from, but not well enough to lend to. A degree of friendship called slight when its object is poor or obscure, and intimate when he is rich or famous.

adherent, *n.*   A follower who has not yet obtained all that he expects to get.

amnesty, *n.*   The state's magnanimity to those offenders whom it would be too expensive to punish.

armor, *n.*   The kind of clothing worn by a man whose tailor is a blacksmith.

barometer, *n.*   An ingenious instrument which indicates what kind of weather we are having.

blackguard, *n.*   A man whose qualities, prepared for display like a box of berries in a market — the fine ones on top — have been opened on the wrong side. An inverted gentleman.

bore, *n.*   A person who talks when you wish him to listen.

boundary, *n.*   In political geography, an imaginary line between two nations, separating the imaginary rights of one from the imaginary rights of the other.

compulsion, *n.*   The eloquence of power.

congratulation, *n.*   The civility of envy.

conservative, *n.*   A statesman who is enamored of existing evils, as distinguished from the Liberal, who wishes to replace them with others.

consult, *v.t.*   To seek another's approval of a course already decided on.

coward, *n.*   One who in a perilous emergency thinks with his legs.

cremona, *n.*   A high-priced violin made in Connecticut.

cynic, *n.*   A blackguard whose faulty vision sees things as they are, not as they ought to be. Hence the custom among the Scythians of plucking out a cynic's eyes to improve his vision.

disobedience, *n.*   The silver lining to the cloud of servitude.

hearse, *n.*   Death's baby-carriage.

historian, *n.* A broad-gauge gossip.

hovel, *n.* The fruit of a flower called the Palace.

immigrant, *n.* An unenlightened person who thinks one country better than another.

kill, *v.t.* To create a vacancy without nominating a successor.

kilt, *n.* A costume sometimes worn by Scotchmen in America and Americans in Scotland.

lawyer, *n.* One skilled in circumvention of the law.

legacy, *n.* A gift from one who is legging it out of this vale of tears.

lighthouse, *n.* A tall building on the seashore in which the government maintains a lamp and the friend of a politician.

majesty, *n.* The state and title of a king. Regarded with a just contempt by the Most Eminent Grand Masters, Grand Chancellors, Great Incohonees and Imperial Potentates of the ancient and honorable orders of republican America.

marriage, *n.* The state or condition of a community consisting of a master, a mistress and two slaves, making in all, two.

mausoleum, *n.* The final and funniest folly of the rich.

Monday, *n.* In Christian countries, the day after the baseball game.

mugwump, *n.* In politics, one afflicted with self-respect and addicted to the vice of independence. A term of contempt.

novel, *n.* A short story padded. A species of composition bearing the same relation to literature that the panorama bears to art. As it is too long to be read at a sitting the impressions made by its successive parts are successively effaced, as in the panorama. Unity, totality of effect, is impossible; for besides the few pages last read all that is carried in mind is the mere plot of what has gone before. To the romance the novel is what photography is to painting. Its distinguishing principle, probability, corresponds to the literal actuality of the photograph and puts it distinctly into the category of reporting; whereas the free wing of the romancer enables him to mount to such altitudes of imagination as he may be fitted to attain; and the first three essentials of the literary art are imagination, imagination and imagination. The art of writing novels, such as it was, is long dead everywhere except in Russia, where is it new. Peace to its ashes—some of which have a large sale.

ocean, *n.*   A body of water occupying about two-thirds of a world made for man—who has no gills.

painting, *n.*   The art of protecting flat surfaces from the weather and exposing them to the critic.

platitude, *n.*   The fundamental element and special glory of popular literature. A thought that snores in words that smoke. The wisdom of a million fools in the diction of a dullard. A fossil sentiment in artificial rock. A moral without the fable. All that is mortal of a

The Devil's Dictionary

89

departed truth. A demi-tasse of milk-and-morality. The Pope's-nose
of a featherless peacock. A jelly-fish withering on the shore of the
sea of thought. The cackle surviving the egg. A desiccated epigram.

politics, *n.*   A strife of interests masquerading as a contest of principles.
The conduct of public affairs for private advantage.

presidency, *n.*   The greased pig in the field game of American politics.

radicalism, *n.*   The conservatism of to-morrow injected into the affairs
of to-day.

un-American, *adj.*   Wicked, intolerable, heathenish.

zigzag, *v.t.*   To move forward uncertainly, from side to side, as one
carrying the white man's burden.

The Princess, the Knight and the Dragon

Stoddard Malarkey

The Princess Miranda went for a stroll,
All on a summer's day—
To pick a flower, to idle an hour,
To rest a bit in a leafy bower,
With a pink umbrella in case of a shower,   5
And a maid to lead the way.

They left the castle far behind,
All on a summer's day—
For the sun was bright, and the air was light,
And they paid no heed to left or right,   10
And they roamed till the castle was out of sight,
And they finally lost their way.

They came to a wood that was gloomy and deep,
All on a summer's day—
"It's the home of Faggon the terrible dragon,   15
With seven long tails and all of them waggin',
And we'd better run home without any laggin',"
The maid was heard to say.

And the maid grew frightened and started to cry,
All on a summer's day—   20
For she had been told the dragon would hold
Damsels for ransom until they grew old,
And would gobble them up if he didn't get gold,
And she hastily scampered away.

The Princess was braver and nobler by far,   25
All on a summer's day—
So she held up her head in spite of her dread,
And though she was frightened no tear did she shed,
And gritting her teeth she courageously said,
"I'll run from no dragons today!"   30

So she went ahead through the gloomy wood,
All on a summer's day—
As she walked along she sang a song,
Of a handsome knight who would come along,
In time to keep Faggon from doing her wrong,   35
And would gallantly save the day.

The Princess,
The Knight
and the Dragon

91

In the heart of the wood, where the wind blew cold,
All on a summer's day—
Where the air was dank and the weeds grew rank,
And the gas from the marshes bubbled and stank,   40
She heard a snort and thump and a clank,
And Faggon stood in her way.

Faggon the Dragon was scaly and green,
All on a summer's day—
His teeth were long and his claws were long,   45
And the fire from his mouth was red and strong,
And on each of his tails was a poisonous prong,
And he carried the Princess away.

The Satiric Voice

Five minutes later, with thunder of hoof,
All on a summer's day—
Up rode the knight, who was geared for the fight,
With his sword in his hand and his helmet on tight,
And his armor all polished and spurs shining bright,
And ready to save the day.

He looked at the tracks the dragon had left,
All on a summer's day—
The wind it made a mournful sound,
The dragon's tracks were large and round,
And the knight turned pale and thoughtfully frowned,
And muttered, "Some other day."

So he rode to the castle to make his report,
All on a summer's day—
He told the king the Princess was dead,
So the king adopted the maid instead,
And the maid and the knight they soon were wed,
And were very merry and gay.

The Princess, however, languished long,
All on a summer's day—
The dragon's dungeon was dank and cold,
And the Princess pined and soon grew old,
And as nobody bothered to send any gold,
The dragon ate her one day.

And so you can see from this tale I tell,
All on a summer's day—
If you ever roam too far from home,
And come across Faggon the terrible dragon,
You'd better run off without any laggin',
And be noble some other day.

*The Princess,
The Knight
and the Dragon*

93

Who and Whom

James Thurber

The number of people who use "whom" and "who" wrongly is appalling. The problem is a difficult one and it is complicated by the importance of tone, or taste. Take the common expression, "Whom are you, anyways?" That is of course, strictly speaking, correct—and yet how formal, how stilted! The usage to be preferred in ordinary speech and writing is "Who are you, anyways?" "Whom" should be used in the nominative case only when a note of dignity or austerity is desired. For example, if a writer is dealing with a meeting of, say, the British Cabinet, it would be better to have the Premier greet a new arrival, such as an under-secretary, with a "Whom are you, anyways?" rather than a "Who are you, anyways?"—always granted that the Premier is sincerely unaware of the man's identity. To address a person one knows by a "Whom are you?" is a mark either of incredible lapse of memory or inexcusable arrogance. "How are you?" is a much kindlier salutation.

The Buried Whom, as it is called, forms a special problem. This is where the word occurs deep in a sentence. For a ready example, take the common expression: "He did not know whether he knew her or not because he had not heard whom the other had said she was until too late to see her." The simplest way out of this is to abandon the "whom" altogether and substitute "where" (a reading of the sentence that way will show how much better it is). Unfortunately, it is only in rare cases that "where" can be used in place of "whom." Nothing could be more flagrantly bad, for instance, than to say "Where are you?" in demanding a person's identity. The only conceivable answer is, "Here I am," which would give no hint at all as to whom the person was. Thus the conversation, or piece of writing, would, from being built upon a false foundation, fall of its own weight.

A common rule for determining whether "who" or "whom" is right is to substitute "she" for "who," and "her" for "whom," and see which sounds the better. Take the sentence, "He met a woman who they said was an actress." Now if "who" is correct then "she" can be used in its place. Let us try it. "He met a woman she they said was an actress." That instantly rings false. It can't be right. Hence the proper usage is "whom."

In certain cases grammatical correctness must often be subordinated to a consideration of taste. For instance, suppose that the same person had met a man whom they said was a street cleaner. The word "whom" is too austere to use in connection with a lowly worker, like a street cleaner, and its use in this form is known as False Admiration or Pathetic Fallacy.

You might say: "There is, then, no hard and fast rule?" ("was then" would be better, since "then" refers to what is past). You might better say, then (or have said): "There was then (or is now) no hard and fast rule?" Only this, that it is better to use "whom" when in doubt, and even better to reword the statement, and leave out all the relative pronouns, except ad, ante, con, in, inter, ob, post, prae, pro, sub, and super.

TO ADDRESS A PERSON ONE KNOWS BY A "WHOM ARE YOU?" IS A
MARK OF INEXCUSABLE ARROGANCE

Who and Whom

Bradbury, Ray, *Farenheit 451*. Ballantine, 1968.

Carroll, Lewis, *Alice's Adventures in Wonderland; Through the Looking Glass*. Macmillan, 1963.

Greene, Graham, *Our Man in Havana*. Bantam, 1968.

Huxley, Aldous, *Brave New World*. Harper & Row, 1932.

Kaufman, Bel, *Up the Down Staircase*. Prentice-Hall, 1964.

McGinley, Phyllis, *Times Three: Selected Poems from Three Decades*. Viking, 1960.

Mencken, H. L., *Bathtub Hoax and Other Blasts and Bravos from the Chicago Tribune*. Knopf, 1958.

Nash, Ogden, *The Pocket Book of Ogden Nash*. Pocket Books, 1962.

Orwell, George, *Animal Farm*. Harcourt Brace Jovanovich, 1954.

_____, *Nineteen Eighty-Four*. Harcourt Brace Jovanovich.

Parkinson, C. Northcote, *Parkinson's Law and Other Studies in Administration*. Ballantine, 1968.

Potter, Stephen, *Gamesmanship, or the Art of Winning Games Without Actually Cheating*. Holt, Rinehart and Winston, 1948.

Rosten, Leo, *The Complete K-a-P-L-a-N*. Harper & Row, 1969.

Thurber, James, *Fables for Our Time*. Harper & Row, 1952.

_____, *Last Flower: A Parable in Pictures*. Harper & Row, 1939.

_____, *Thurber Carnival*. Harper & Row, 1945.

Twain, Mark, *A Connecticut Yankee in King Arthur's Court*. Harcourt Brace Jovanovich, 1962.

_____, *Pudd'nhead Wilson*. Harcourt Brace Jovanovich, 1962.

About the Authors

Stephen Vincent Benét (1898–1943) *American author*
Stephen Vincent Benét's interest in writing and in the American past were both part of his family heritage. Educated at Yale and the Sorbonne, he had his first literary success with the *Ballad of William Sycamore* (1923). This was followed five years later by his epic-ballad dealing with the Civil War, *John Brown's Body*. It was a romantic treatment of a period which is always of interest to Americans. *John Brown's Body* received the Pulitzer Prize for poetry in 1929. Benét's short stories are often rooted in American history, as are many of his novels, much of his poetry, and his librettos for two folk-operas.

e. e. cummings (1894–1962) *American poet*
Edward Estlin Cummings was educated at Harvard, to which he later returned as a Charles Eliot Norton Professor. In the interval he became one of the most innovative of American poets, with a body of verse that flagrantly violated every dictum of formal poetry except the fundamental dictum of creating a verse so magnetically alive that few readers can escape its spell. Grammar, spelling, and punctuation were forced into a new mode by this poet who defied the conventions of language and explored new possibilities for poetic expression.

Shirley Jackson (1919–1965) *American novelist and short story writer*
Born in San Francisco, Shirley Jackson spent much of her adult life in a rural community in Vermont where she and her husband, literary critic Stanley Edgar Hymen, continued their literary careers. Although she wrote a number of novels, some dealing with the deeper levels of human consciousness (*The Bird's Nest*) and others with the humor of family life (*Life Among the Savages*), she is probably best known for her strange and chilling story "The Lottery," which has been frequently anthologized and even dramatized for television.

Robinson Jeffers (1887–1962) *American poet*
After years of restless and desultory study and work, Robinson Jeffers settled down to a life of poetry in 1914. From this time on, he lived a secluded life in Carmel, California, in a house built with his own hands, writing poems of the Big Sur country which stretched around him. Austere, powerful, pessimistic, Robinson Jeffers has something redolent of Greek tragedy in both his life and his work. For him civilization is a "transient disease," and man himself a "needless" animal on the face of an otherwise beautiful earth. Jeffers became a well-known figure when his "free adaptation" of Euripides' *Medea* became a Broadway success in 1947.

Archibald MacLeish (1892–) *American poet*
Although Archibald MacLeish has filled major positions in many fields, his reputation seems most secure as a poet. After a few years of unhappy practice as a lawyer, he went with his wife and children to live in Paris, where, as he says, "I date the beginning of my life." Here he read and wrote in earnest and after his return to America received his first Pulitzer Prize in 1932. In 1949, MacLeish bcame Boyleston professor of rhetoric and oratory at Harvard. In 1952 his *Collected Poems* won him a second Pulitzer Prize. *J. B.*, a verse drama which is based on the biblical story of Job and explores the problem of human suffering, won for MacLeish a third Pulitzer Prize.

Diane Oliver (1943–1966) *American short story writer*
The promising literary career of Diane Oliver came to a tragic end when she was killed in an automobile accident at the age of twenty-three. She had graduated from the University of North Carolina and was a student at the Writer's Workshop at the University of Iowa at the time of her death. Herself a Negro, she frequently wrote about Negro life

in her native South, and her short stories have been widely published. "Neighbors" was selected for inclusion in *Prize Stories of 1967: O. Henry Awards*.

Alastair Reid   (1926–   )   *British poet*
The son of a Scottish minister, Reid graduated with honors from St. Andrews University. After having served in the Royal Navy, he came to the United States, where for four years he was a professor at Sarah Lawrence College. During that time, his first volume of poems, *To Lighten My House*, was published in 1953. Mr. Reid, who spends half of every year traveling, is currently a staff writer for the *New Yorker* and a contributor to *Encounter* and the *Atlantic Monthly*.

Sophocles   (ca. 496–406 B.C.)   *Greek dramatist*
Sophocles is one of the three great dramatists—Aeschylus and Euripides being the others—of the Golden Age of Greek drama. "Rich, handsome, and good-natured," he gives the lie to the theory that great tragedy must be born from personal tragedy. During his lifetime Athens was at the height of her glory, well able to nurture and subsidize the arts, and Sophocles was spared both poverty and insecurity. He is supposed to have written over a hundred plays, of which only seven are still extant. Of these the most famous is *Antigone*, which explores conflict between personal conscience and the good of the state. Such a theme is obviously a perennial concern and as a result *Antigone* has been frequently adapted to the needs of almost every age.

Henry David Thoreau   (1817–1862)   *American essayist and naturalist*
A friend and disciple of Ralph Waldo Emerson, Thoreau is an incarnation of Emerson's theory of individuality. Considered an eccentric in his own day, Thoreau has been more kindly treated by posterity. Feeling, as he himself phrased it, that "society is always diseased, and the best is the most so," Thoreau determined to live in society as little as possible. His most famous work, *Walden*, was written during the two years that he left Concord for the woods around Walden Pond in order, as he put it, to "live deliberately." Thoreau was essentially a naturalist who possessed keen and patient powers of observation which enabled him to see the most minute aspects of nature.

About the Authors

Index of Authors and Titles

Illustration Credits

p. 3 The Metropolitan Museum of Art, Carnavon Collection. Gift of Edward S. Harkness, 1926.
pp. 5–46 The Repertory Theatre of Lincoln Center Production. Photographs by Martin Swope.
p. 53 Holt, Rinehart and Winston, Inc.
pp. 56–57 Culver Pictures
p. 67 The New York Public Library
pp. 76–77 Sonja Bullaty-Romeo (Rapho Guillumette)